"The world was peopled
with wonders."

The origin of Wildsam comes from above, a
line of prose in the novel, *East of Eden*, written by
John Steinbeck. Six words hinting at a broad and
interwoven idea. One of curiosity, connection, joy. And
the belief that stories have the power to unearth the
mysteries of a place—for anyone. The book in
your hands is rooted in such things.

D1286239

Our deepest gratitude to everyone in New Orleans who helped us
create this second-edition city guide. Special thanks goes to the
Historic New Orleans Collection, The Hogan Archive of New
Orleans Music and New Orleans Jazz at Tulane, and New Orleans
Public Library; Nathalie Jordi, Char Thian Miller, Kristian
Sonnier, David Olasky, Kate LeSueur, Samantha Alviani, Sara
Roahen, Chris Hannah, Brett Anderson and Alex Lebow for
steering us in right directions; Anthony DelRosario, for Lester's
story; Rien Fertel, Katy Reckdahl and L. Kasimu Harris, for great
storytelling; and Scott Campbell, for stunning illustrations.

WILDSAM FIELD GUIDES™

Copyright © 2021

Published in the United States
by Wildsam Field Guides, Austin, Texas.

ISBN 978-1-4671-9961-2

Illustrations by Scott Campbell

To find more field guides, please visit
www.wildsam.com

CONTENTS

*Discover the people and places
that tell the story of New Orleans*

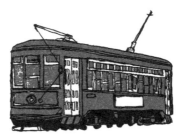

WELCOME

———

THERE IS NO OTHER CITY with its own soundtrack like New Orleans. Its people know every word by heart. Those verses and choruses, calls and responses reverberate deep in their bones like a choir singing out into the nave of one of the city's ancient, fern-fuzzed churches.

The Treme Brass Band wailing "Grazing in the Grass" under the rainbow ceiling of Vaughan's Lounge; a Mardi Gras Indian tribe chanting "Here Dey Come" during a second line; Rebirth Brass Band clapping along to "Do Watcha Wanna" on a Thursday night at The Howlin' Wolf; Shannon Powell and Jason Marsalis playing Professor Longhair's "Big Chief" on a front porch for neighbors in folding chairs; James Booker's "Junco Partner" coming through a speaker playing WWOZ 90.7 FM; and the Preservation Hall Jazz Band carrying the dirge of "Saint James Infirmary Blues" within the hall's weathered walls. The album of the city continues to spin no matter how many times the needle scratches or the belt breaks. The rhythms of Congo Square and jazz ghost Buddy Bolden on his cornet still echo through it all.

New Orleanians have an effusive joy that can't be contained, like deep summer rainwater underneath those moon-and-stars-emblazoned manhole covers. Here, people step out of their cars in the middle of a street to dance, funerals are parades and the neighborhood bar stage is as holy as a cathedral pulpit.

Yet sometimes, all the singing, dancing and laughing is to keep from crying. New Orleans is so easy and so hard to love. There's the croon of a clarinet from a street band, heady spring jasmine blooms, cottages in every color of the crayon box, the first soul-warming spoonful of gumbo. But for all the beauty in New Orleans, there are the unhealed wounds of institutional racism and Hurricane Katrina evident—in swollen prisons and displaced generational residents. The roads are crumbling. The pumps that keep the city afloat seem to run on wishes and prayers.

Perhaps the confluence is found in an old Creole proverb: "Tell me who you love and I'll tell you who you are." New Orleanians will tell you they love their city even through the tireless work to fix its flaws. They love the people who make this incomparable place play on against all odds. Listen to their stories and their songs. —The Editors

ESSENTIALS

TRANSPORT

STREETCAR
St. Charles Streetcar Line
norta.com

BIKES
Alex's Bikes
alexsbikes.com

LANDMARKS

ST. LOUIS CATHEDRAL
Jackson Square
Oldest cathedral in the U.S.

CRESCENT PARK BRIDGE
Piety St and Chartres St
Modern but patinaed archway
into city's riverside park.

MERCEDES-BENZ SUPERDOME
1500 *Sugar Bowl Dr*
Mothership stadium a spiritual
home for Saints fans. A "shelter of
last resort" during Katrina.

MEDIA

RADIO
WWOZ 90.7 FM
Globally loved community station.

DIGITAL NEWSLETTER
The Boil Advisory
Biweekly food news and stories.

ALT NEWSPAPER
Antigravity
Deep political, cultural coverage.

GREENSPACE

CITY PARK
1 *Palm Dr*
Covers 1,300 acres dotted by
600-year-old live oaks and
bordered by bayous. Contains
an urban farm, sculpture walk,
wildflower field, botanical
garden, art museum and more.

FOODWAY

PO'BOY
Crusty French bread piled with
roast beef, fried seafood, smoked
sausage, etc. Get it "dressed" with
lettuce, tomato, pickle and mayo.

CALENDAR

JAN - APR
Krewe de Jeanne d'Arc Parade
Mardi Gras
Super Sunday

MAY- AUG
Jazz & Heritage Festival
Satchmo Summerfest
Southern Decadence

SEP - DEC
Saints Season Opener
Tremé Creole Gumbo Festival
Celebration in the Oaks

BOOKS
☞ *The Yellow House*
   by Sarah M. Broom
☞ *The Moviegoer* by Walker Percy
☞ *Why New Orleans Matters*
   by Tom Piazza

FRIDAY

Morning jog on St. Charles
   streetcar tracks
Early dinner at Upperline
Live music at Maple Leaf Bar

....

SATURDAY

Breakfast gumbo at Bywater Bakery
New Orleans Jazz Museum
Courtyard drinks at Cane & Table

....

SUNDAY

Brunch at Cafe Degas
Walk through sculpture garden at
   City Park
Sno-balls at Hansen's Sno-Bliz

MEMENTOS

More Jazz T-shirt, *DNO*, $30
Spicy Satsuma jam, *Jamboree Jams*, $10
Signed Jazz & Heritage Festival poster, *Art4Now*, $400

RECORD COLLECTION

Allen Toussaint	*Southern Nights*
The Meters	*Cabbage Alley*
Dr. John	*In the Right Place*
James Booker	*Classified*
Mahalia Jackson	*Bless This House*
Cha Wa	*My People*
Louis Armstrong	*Ella and Louis*
Irma Thomas	*Soul Queen of New Orleans*
Juvenile	*400 Degreez*
Jon Batiste	*WE ARE*
Professor Longhair	*New Orleans Piano*
The Neville Brothers	*Fiyo on the Bayou*
Fats Domino	*Fats Domino Swings*
Ellis Marsalis	*On the First Occasion*

ESSENTIALS

Hotel Peter & Paul
2317 Burgundy St
A long-shuttered
Catholic church and
school resurrected as
a French country- and
Creole-inspired respite.

....

Maison de la Luz
546 Carondelet St
Details designed by
Studio Shamshiri
abound, like a secret
cocktail window and
serpentine handles.

....

The Roosevelt
130 Roosevelt Way
Sip the namesake of the
Sazerac bar, an art deco
gem, lobby-level.

....

Hotel Saint Vincent
1507 Magazine St
A Liz Lambert joint.
Sprawling Italianate
manor [once an or-
phanage] imbued with
'70s glam.

....

The Chloe
4125 St Charles Ave
A moody blue-hued
mansion with 14 luxe
rooms. Pool scene.

Travelers
1476 Magazine St
A mod nine-room
B&B in the middle of
the historic Garden
District. Run by artist
co-op that lives on-site.
They even made the
headboards.

....

The Old No. 77 Hotel
535 Tchoupitoulas St
Former coffee ware-
house in Central Busi-
ness District. Home to
chef Nina Compton's
Caribbean brasserie,
Compère Lapin.

....

Columns
3811 St Charles Ave
St. Charles Avenue
fixture just had a major
makeover. Listen to
the streetcar rumble
by in the velvety down-
stairs parlor.

....

Soniat House Hotel
1133 Chartres St
You needn't sacrifice
a solid eight to stay
in the Quarter at this
charming 1830s town
house turned inn.

HEY! Coffee Co.
Mid-City

....

Pond
Marigny

....

Coffee Science
Mid-City

....

Mammoth
Espresso
CBD

....

Petite Clouet Café
Bywater

Octavia Books
Uptown

....

Blue Cypress
Books
Carrollton

....

Beckham's
Bookshop
French Quarter

....

Garden District
Book Shop
Garden District

....

Crescent City
Books
French Quarter

ISSUES

Potholes	New Orleans potholes are comically bad. Just follow Instagram account @lookatthisfuckinstreet to see how residents enshrine particularly cavernous ones. Jokes aside, crumbling roadways plague every part of the city. The affluent Audubon and economically disadvantaged Lower Ninth Ward neighborhoods both received F grades on their streets in a recent city assessment. **EXPERT:** *Amy Glovinsky, CEO, Bureau of Governmental Research*
Charter Schools	After Hurricane Katrina in 2005, New Orleans' dysfunctional public school system was replaced entirely with a charter school model. Scores have improved, but many schools still underperform compared with the state average. **EXPERT:** *Douglas N. Harris, director, Education Research Alliance for New Orleans*
Flooding	Despite a complex system of pumps and turbines, heavy rain regularly floods the city and ruptured water mains prompt boil advisories. Progressive infrastructure design [like porous paving] and federal funding could alleviate future issues. **EXPERT:** *David Waggonner, director, Greater New Orleans Urban Water Plan*
Youth Incarceration	A spike in youth crime became a leading issue in Orleans Parish's 2020 district attorney race. Almost all youth arrests are Black children who, in some cases, still face life sentences. **EXPERT:** *Teneé Felix, juvenile division chief, Orleans Parish District Attorney's Office*

STATISTICS

390,144 .... Current residents, 81 percent of pre-Hurricane Katrina pop.

4 .... St. Augustine HS alumni nominated for Grammys in 2021

1934 ....Year Hansen's Sno-Bliz's ice shaving machine was built

21 .... Neighborhoods on National Register of Historic Places

24% .... New Orleans' poverty rate, double the national average

19.75 million .... Tourists who visited New Orleans in 2019

800 ....Estimated age in years of oldest live oak in City Park

NEIGHBORHOODS

MARIGNY-BYWATER

Technicolor cottages, cafes, corner stores and dives galore. Its DIY spirit shows in porch pop-ups, craft markets, public art.

LOCAL: *Budsi's Authentic Thai, Hi-Ho Lounge, Frady's One Stop*

....

BAYOU ST. JOHN

Tucked between Mid-City and its namesake waterway where locals paddle and picnic. It's surrounded by some of the city's oldest homes.

LOCAL: *Parkway Bakery & Tavern, Cansesco's, 1000 Figs*

....

IRISH CHANNEL

Sandwiched between the river and the Garden District. Both its working-class residents and ancient live oaks have deep roots here, but this close-knit corner is drawing more newcomers too.

LOCAL: *Molly's Rise & Shine, Parasol's, Urban Roots*

....

CENTRAL CITY

The beating heart of local culture, from second lines to the smell of Leidenheimer bread. Momentous civil rights history.

LOCAL: *Heard Dat Kitchen, Verret's Lounge, Café Reconcile*

TREMÉ

One of the country's oldest Black neighborhoods and the wellspring of many jazz and brass band greats.

LOCAL: *Little People's Place, Saint Augustine Catholic Church*

....

LOWER GARDEN DISTRICT

Anchored by a bustling shopping section at iron-balconied Magazine Street and Coliseum Square, a shady, go-to green space.

LOCAL: *The Courtyard Brewery, Commander's Palace, Hivolt*

....

CARROLLTON

So far uptown it feels like its own village, especially on main drag Oak Street. Also sees ebb and flow of nearby university students.

LOCAL: *Coutelier NOLA, Snake and Jake's Christmas Club Lounge, Bellegarde Bakery*

....

FRENCH QUARTER

What tourists see as a decorum-be-damned playground, locals know is foremost a neighborhood. Keep that perspective to uncover its true treasures. Reverence is rewarded.

LOCAL: *Manolito, C'Mere, Cabrini Playground, Peychaud's Bar*

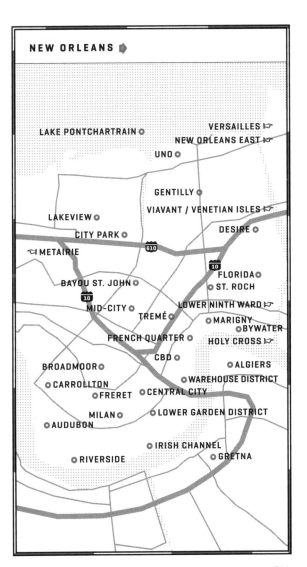

NEW ORLEANS

LAKE PONTCHARTRAIN
VERSAILLES
NEW ORLEANS EAST
UNO
GENTILLY
VIAVANT / VENETIAN ISLES
LAKEVIEW
DESIRE
CITY PARK
METAIRIE
610
10
FLORIDA
BAYOU ST. JOHN
ST. ROCH
10
MID-CITY
LOWER NINTH WARD
TREMÉ
MARIGNY
BYWATER
FRENCH QUARTER
HOLY CROSS
CBD
BROADMOOR
ALGIERS
WAREHOUSE DISTRICT
CARROLLTON
FRERET
CENTRAL CITY
MILAN
LOWER GARDEN DISTRICT
AUDUBON
IRISH CHANNEL
RIVERSIDE
GRETNA

BESTS

A curated list of city favorites—classic and
new—from bars and restaurants to shops and experiences,
plus a handful of can't-miss experts

FOOD & DRINK

*For maps of Classic Cuisine and Drinking Spots,
see pages 56 and 68.*

NEIGHBORHOOD CAFE

Bywater Bakery

3624 Dauphine St
Bywater

Corner congregation spot for breakfast gumbo, cookies and live music. Best king cake contender.

....

OYSTERS

Casamento's

4330 Magazine St
Touro

Chartreuse-and-teal-tiled shoebox from another time [1919]. The order: oyster loaf and chargrilled fries.

....

SNO-BALL

Hansen's Sno-Bliz

4801 Tchoupitoulas St
Uptown

Velvet ice drenched in housemade syrups. Yes, it's worth the wait. No, this isn't a snow cone. You'll see.

PO'BOY

Domilise's

5240 Annunciation St
Uptown

Longtime family-owned favorite. Large meatball, bag of Zapp's and a Barq's root beer.

....

COCKTAILS

Cure

4905 Freret St
Freret

Responsible for the city's cocktail renaissance. The list is long, but the daily punch is always strong.

....

VIETNAMESE

Tan Dinh

1705 Lafayette St
Gretna

Drive over the river to the West Bank for pho, hot-and-sour catfish and lemongrass frog legs.

CLASSIC

Upperline

1413 Upperline St
Uptown

Covered with owner JoAnn Clevenger's art collection. Spicy shrimp and cornbread a must.

....

MODERN CAJUN

Mosquito Supper Club

3824 Dryades St
Milan

Melissa Martin serves a meal that tells a story about her roots in fishing village Chauvin.

....

COFFEE SHOP

Pagoda Café

1430 N Dorgenois St
Seventh Ward

Beloved Bayou Road-corridor oasis now leading by example as a worker-owned co-op.

CREOLE SOUL

Li'l Dizzy's Cafe
1500 Esplanade Ave
Seventh Ward
Reopened by popular demand. Red beans on Monday. Fried chicken all the time.

....

FISH PLATE

Barrow's Catfish
8300 Earhart Blvd
Gert Town
Crispy curled fillets a Lenten staple.

....

GELATO

Angelo Brocato
214 N Carrollton Ave
Mid-City
Since 1905. Cannoli, biscotti, torta ricotta.

....

TAPAS & WINE

Bacchanal Wine
600 Poland Ave
Bywater
Courtyard party. Well-rounded bottle list, pick-your-own cheese plates, live jazz.

....

GUMBO

Neyow's Creole Café
3332 Bienville St
Mid-City
Soul-warming shrimp-ham-sausage combo for those cold yet humid winter days.

CHICKEN WINGS

Manchu Food Store
1413 N Claiborne Ave
Tremé
Purple-painted convenience store. Chinese food, liquor too.

....

BREAD & PASTRY

Levee Baking Co.
3138 Magazine St
Irish Channel
Seasonally influenced. Sells out quickly. Strawberry morning buns, olive oil cookies, challah.

....

HONDURAN

Alma
800 Louisa St
Bywater
Melissa Araujo shares family recipes in her own distinct way.

....

ITALIAN

Paladar 511
511 Marigny St
Marigny
Cali-Italian menu with a focus on veggies.

....

HAITIAN

Fritai
1535 Basin St
Tremé
Charly Pierre connects Haitian and New Orleans dishes.

SANDWICHES

Turkey and the Wolf
739 Jackson Ave
Irish Channel
Unapologetically unserious. Lunch only except Friday night special.

....

PIZZA

Pizza Delicious
617 Piety St
Bywater
Locals line up for simple yet sophisticated pies and pasta.

....

BAR SNACKS

Coquette
2800 Magazine St
Irish Channel
Fancy roe-topped onion dip with an expert cocktail.

....

SEAFOOD

Pêche
800 Magazine St
CBD
The best anywhere for enjoying the fruits of the Gulf.

....

MARGARITA GARDEN

Barracuda
3984 Tchoupitoulas St
Touro
Hip hangout for nacho happy hour, fresh frozens.

SHOPPING

BOUTIQUE

St. Claude Social Club
1933 Sophie Wright Pl
LGD
Like shopping the closets of New Orleans' most stylish. Color, statement jewelry, breezy fabrics rule here.

....

JEWISH DELI

Stein's Market & Deli
2207 Magazine St
Irish Channel
Lawyer turned deli-owner Dan Stein is equally perfectionist and punk. Bagels, tinned fish, knishes.

....

ANTIQUES

M.S. Rau
622 Royal St
French Quarter
A 40,000 sq. ft. show-room for serious shop-pers with a sapphires and silver budget.

BOOKSHOP

Faulkner House Books
624 Pirate's Alley
French Quarter
Alley hideaway feels akin to wandering the private library of a Creole town house.

....

HOMETOWN PRIDE

DNO
1101 First St
Garden District
Home of Defend New Orleans tees, also partners with local organizations supporting NOLA culture and workers.

....

WINE

The Independent Caveau NOLA
1226 S White St
Gert Town
Skinny warehouse in an industrial area conceals a cheese and natural-wine cache.

VINYL

Domino Sound Record Shack
1557 Bayou Rd
Seventh Ward
Crate diggers come for the incredible collection of world, traditional and NOLA-made music.

....

GARDEN

Harold's Plants
1135 Press St
Bywater
Tropical trove hidden behind the railroad tracks. Jake, Sammy and Eddie a few of the nursery cats.

....

HEIRLOOM COOKWARE

Seasoned
3828 Dryades St
Milan
From collectibles to kitsch. Vintage Pyrex, cast iron, juice glasses, copper pots.

VINTAGE

Blue Dream

2121 *Chartres St*
Marigny

Edited racks alongside locally made jewelry and curious objects.

....

BLACK LITERATURE

Baldwin & Co.

1030 *Elysian Fields*
Ave, Marigny

Coffee shop and bookstore focused on Black authors, plus a podcast studio and patio.

....

BUTCHER SHOP

Piece of Meat

3301 *Bienville St*
Mid-City

Full-service counter for regionally raised cuts. Sandwiches too.

....

WIGS

Fifi Mahony's

934 *Royal St*
French Quarter

Custom creations for Mardi Gras or a typical Tuesday.

....

PAPER RELICS

Arcadian Books & Prints

714 *Orleans St*
French Quarter

Stack sifters may just strike gold.

MEN'S STYLE

Rubensteins

102 *St Charles Ave*
CBD

Old-school department store from 1924. Roberto and Ozzie will set you up.

....

FURNITURE

Merchant House

1150 *Magazine St*
LGD

A contemporary-style antiques mall. Look for vendors like Vice & Graft.

....

VICTORIAN TILE

Derby Pottery & Tile

2029 *Magazine St*
LGD

Maker of street-name tile replicas.

....

ART GALLERY

Fawkes Fine Art

940 *Royal St*
French Quarter

Pink parlor for some of the city's brightest emerging artists.

....

HOME GOODS

Sunday Shop

2025 *Magazine St*
LGD

Pieces that set a scene, from all eras and traditions.

MAGICAL TOOLS

Crescent City Conjure

2402 *Royal St*
Marigny

All things hoodoo, rootwork and witchcraft.

....

HATS

Meyer the Hatter

120 *St Charles Ave*
CBD

Largest hat shop in the South, since 1894.

....

ARCHITECTURAL SALVAGE

Ricca's

511 *N Solomon St*
Mid-City

Preserver and dealer of demolition finds, from doors to stained glass to faucet handles.

....

SUMMERWEAR

Lekha

shoplekha.com

Designer Trishala Bhansali's lightweight, Indian-inspired garments perfect for steamy weather.

....

STATIONERY

Scriptura

5423 *Magazine St*
Uptown

Couture letterpress and engraving work.

ACTION

For maps of Mardi Gras and Historic Homes,
see pages 60 and 72.

TRADITIONAL JAZZ
Preservation Hall
726 St Peter
French Quarter
A sacred space for America's original art form. Ben Jaffe carries on his parents' mission to preserve it.
....

RUNNING
Audubon Park
6500 Magazine St
Audubon
A 2-mile paved loop under Spanish moss-draped oaks, past ponds dotted with beautiful birds.
....

CEMETERY TOUR
Save Our Cemeteries
saveourcemeteries.org
Nonprofit both preserves city's iconic aboveground tombs and provides moving, factual tours.

PADDLE
Bayou St. John
Magnolia Bridge
Bayou St. John
An urban waterway and favorite weekend respite for locals. Turns into a party during Bayou Boogaloo and Mardi Gras.
....

MUSIC HISTORY
A Closer Walk
acloserwalknola.com
Take a self-guided pilgrimage to important sites, past and present, humble and grand, of New Orleans' music canon.
....

MARDI GRAS INDIANS
Backstreet Cultural Museum
1116 Henriette Delille
Tremé
The Francis family's shrine to the city's most unique culture.

ART MUSEUM
The Ogden
925 Camp St
CBD
Impressive collection of the South's best artists, especially folk art, from Howard Finster to Clementine Hunter.
....

COOKING CLASS
The Bakehouse
thebakehousenola.com
Join Joy Wilson, a.k.a. Joy the Baker, in her Bywater cottage and learn how to make pie, cookies and Drake on Cake.
....

FESTIVAL
New Orleans Jazz & Heritage Festival
Fair Grounds Race Course [April/May]
Two weeks of revelry and reunion. Major headliners, local greats.

OUTDOOR THEATER

The Broadside
600 N Broad St
Mid-City
The Broad's sister
venue shows movies
and music alfresco.
Full bar too.

....

BRASS FOR HIRE

Kinfolk Brass Band
neworleanskinfolk.com
Spiced-up standards
for parades, block
parties, weddings,
whenever.

....

POP-UP DINNER

Dakar Nola
@dakarnola
Serigne Mbaye's
Senegalese Creole
suppers.

....

STATE PARK

Fontainebleau State
Park
62883 Hwy 1089
Mandeville
North shore nature
escape beloved by
birders.

....

LOCAL VOICES

Neighborhood
Story Project
2202 Lapeyrouse St
Seventh Ward
Community exhibi-
tions, conversations.

HISTORY MUSEUM

Le Musée de f.p.c.
2336 Esplanade Ave
Seventh Ward
Historic house
museum explores
compelling, compli-
cated history of free
people of color.

....

GYM

New Orleans
Athletic Club
222 N Rampart St
Tremé
Grand Budapest
Hotel–like interior
with eclectic clientele.

....

BOUNCE CLASS

Dancing Grounds
dancinggrounds.org
Learn the moves and
release your wiggle at
Crescent Park.

....

DAY TRIP

Lafayette, LA
[*135 miles*]
The heart of Aca-
diana, Louisiana's
Cajun country.

....

FARMERS MARKET

Crescent City
Farmers Market
Citywide
Line up early during
citrus, fig and straw-
berry seasons.

PARK PICNIC

Coliseum Square
1708 Coliseum St
LGD
A Seurat-looking
Sunday afternoon,
just with more go-
cups and a jazz band.

....

AUCTION HOUSE

Neal Auction
Company
4038 Magazine St
Touro
Specializes in fine
art and Southern
antiques.

....

GAY BAR

Golden Lantern
1239 Royal St
French Quarter
Home base for city's
Southern Decadence
parade.

....

NBA GAME

Smoothie King
Center
1501 Dave Dixon Dr
CBD
Witness the
Pelicans' Zion era.

....

LIVE CRAWFISH

Captain Sid's
1700 Lake Ave
Bucktown
The best for a back-
yard boil.

EXPERTISE

BIOGRAPHER

Walter Isaacson

@WalterIsaacson

New Orleans–born Tulane University history professor. Has chronicled Jobs, Einstein, Franklin and Kissinger.

....

GRASSROOTS KREWE

Devin De Wulf

redbeansparade.com

Krewe of Red Beans founder started efforts that raised $2 million over 2020 for culture bearers, neighborhood bars.

....

INDIGENOUS HISTORY

Jeffery U. Darensbourg

@hoktiwe

Writes about state's Native community and history. Creator of zine *Bulbancha Is Still a Place*.

PUBLIC ART

Brandan "BMike" Odums

bmike.com

Hand and mind behind city's vivid murals of Buddy Bolden, Travis Hill. HQ at Studio Be in Bywater.

....

DJ

Melissa A. Weber

djsoulsister.com

Better known as DJ Soul Sister. Hosts WWOZ 90.7 FM show and dance parties at spots like the Hi-Ho Lounge.

....

POET

Tiana Nobile

tiananobile.com

Nationally acclaimed talent. Latest collection *Cleave* ponders the history of transnational adoption, including her own.

FRENCH BREAD

Sandy Whann

leidenheimer.com

Fourth-generation owner of 125-year-old bakery considered the gold-standard producer of po'boy bread.

....

BLACKSMITH

Darryl Reeves

neworleansblacksmith.net

Seventh-Ward forger of graceful cast-iron gates, fences and railings. Oft seen at Garden District homes and churches.

....

ANTIQUES

Andrew Hopkins

@boyneworleans1850

Painter, drag queen and self-described bon vivant, also well-regarded as a collector of American and European treasures.

TRANSGENDER RIGHTS
Mariah Moore
houseoftulip.org
Transgender Law Center organizer works on both hyper-local needs and big policy changes.
....

TAROT
Michelle Embree
michelleembree.com
Readings via email; produces podcast too.
....

FLORIST
Sara Perez-Ekanger
antiguafloral.com
Arrangements echo hues of both New Orleans' patinaed and saturated sides.
....

BURLESQUE
Kitten N' Lou
kittenandlou.com
Couple stages performances in Bywater backyard by night. Slings Chance in Hell SnoBalls on front porch by day.
....

HOUSELESS COMMUNITY
Southern Solidarity
southernsolidarity.org
Volunteer group provides food, shelter and medicine for city's housing insecure.

VOTER INFORMATION
Antigravity
antigravitymagazine.com
Monthly news magazine provides extensive guides to help residents navigate local and state choices.
....

PRESERVATION
Danielle Del Sol
prcno.org
Leader of resource center dedicated to saving architecture.
....

HOSPITALITY REFORM
Lauren Darnell
minofoundation.org
Nonprofit director implements programs to build a more equitable hospitality industry.
....

JAZZ INSTRUCTION
NOCCA
nocca.com
Alumni: Wynton Marsalis, Trombone Shorty, Harry Connick Jr.
....

YA-KA-MEIN
Linda Green
neworleanssoulfood.com
Guardian of the stew. Noodle soup also called "Old Sober."

RESEARCH LIBRARY
The Historic New Orleans Collection
hnoc.org
French Quarter athenaeum houses full range of materials to understand city's place in history.
....

MARCHING BAND
St. Augustine HS
staugnola.org
The "Marching 100" recently featured on Jon Batiste's album opener "WE ARE."
....

MULTILINGUAL MUSIC
Leyla McCalla
leylamccalla.com
Reinterprets traditionals. Sings in French, Haitian Creole and English.
....

PHOTOGRAPHY
Akasha Rabut
@akasharabut
Captures urban cowboys, motorcycle clubs and Mardi Gras Indian tribes.
....

COASTAL RESILIENCE
Steve Cochran
mississippiriverdelta.org
Campaign director for Restore the Mississippi River Delta coalition.

MORE THAN 30 ENTRIES ↦
Excerpts have been edited for clarity and concision.

ALMANAC

A deep dive into the cultural heritage of New Orleans
through timelines, how-tos, newspaper clippings, letters,
lists, jazz reviews and other historical hearsay

JAZZ GREATS

Instrument	Player
Tuba	Anthony Lacen
Trombone	Honoré Dutrey, Kid Ory
Cornet	Joe "King" Oliver, Buddy Bolden
Alto Horn	Isidore Barbarin
Mellophone	Davey Jones
Trumpet	Louis Armstrong, Terence Blanchard
Piccolo Trumpet	Wynton Marsalis
Pocket Trumpet	Gary Bruce Hirstius
Baritone	Paul Crawford
Alto Sax	Donald Harrison
Tenor Sax	Johnny Pennino
Soprano Sax	Sidney Bechet
Sousaphone	Philip Frazier
Piano	Champion Jack Dupree, Allen Toussaint
Clarinet	Barney Bigard
Bass	George "Pops" Foster
Banjo	Johnny St. Cyr
Drums	Louis Cottrell Sr., Warren "Baby" Dodds
Composition	Jelly Roll Morton

RAMOS GIN FIZZ

First shaken [and shaken and shaken] by Henry Ramos in the late 1800s at his bar on Gravier Street, the fizzy NOLA concoction traditionally took 12 minutes to make. In his heydey, Ramos had 20 working barmen shaking them at a time. Below, a classic recipe.

- ⮞ 1 teaspoon powdered sugar
- ⮞ 1 jigger gin
- ⮞ Juice ½ lemon and ½ lime
- ⮞ 1 egg white
- ⮞ 3 oz. orange flower water
- ⮞ 1 ounce sweet cream

Combine seven ingredients in a shaker without ice and shake for one minute. Add ice and shake again for at least a couple of minutes [all 12 if you have it in you]. Strain and serve in eight-ounce glass. Fill up with soda water.

ARCHITECTURAL DETAIL

Term	Description
Abat-Vent	*roof extension, almost flat, cantilevered from the facade*
Alligatoring	*severe cracking and crazing of paint*
Appliqué	*applied ornamentation*
Bousillage	*construction method for walls using mixture of mud and moss between heavy timber posts*
Camelback Shotgun	*shotgun type house with a two-story rear portion; also called a "Humpback"*
Colombage	*popular framing method in early colonial period using timber mortised and tenoned together*
Creole Cottage	*French Quarter house style in 1800s, as seen in Lafitte's Blacksmith Shop*
Double Gallery	*two-story houses with a side-gabled or hipped roof, asymmetrical facade*
Egg-and-Dart	*decorative molding alternating between egg- and dart-shaped elements*
Faubourg	*French word meaning suburb*
Finial	*topping ornament of a roof gable, turret, baluster or post*
Foot-Candle	*the illumination unit produced by a source of one candle at a distance of one foot*
Garçonnière	*Creole outbuilding used as living quarters for the young gentleman of the house*
Hipped Roof	*roof with four uniformly sloped sides; maisonette*
Modillions	*small bracket-like ornamentation under the cornice of a classical entablature*
Parapets	*portion of a wall that projects above an adjacent roof surface*
Porte Cochère	*carriage- or passageway providing access to rear courtyard*
Quoin	*stone, brick, or wood block used to accentuate the outside corners of a building*

FABULOUS NEW ORLEANS

Lyle Saxon, noted Louisiana writer and historian, published this
timeless work in 1928. And, in addition, he commandeered the
Federal Writers' Project WPA guide to the city in the late 1930s.
A good friend and generous host to visiting literati [John Steinbeck
was married in Saxon's French Quarter town house], and himself
an unsatisfied novelist, Mr. Saxon was [and is] a beloved reporter
of New Orleans enchantment. Below, an excerpt from Fabulous
New Orleans.

We did not return through the square, but went down some narrow street leading away from the river, toward the center of the old city. The sunlight was sliding down the walls, and in the open windows and doors women were gossiping. Parrots in cages hanging in upper windows screamed with raucous voices. Boys whistled as they passed carrying baskets. Heavy doors swung wide on protesting hinges, showing long dark passages with sunlit courtyards beyond, where flowers grew and festoons of vines clung to mouldering walls. As we passed through the streets the negro women were washing the banquettes by the simple expedient of pouring pails of water in great swishes, careless of the legs of passers-by. Other negro women were scrubbing staircases with pounded brick dust—"reddenin'" they called it. An old negro woman passed by, dressed in blue and wearing a stiff white apron. She carried a covered basket and as she walked she cried monotonously: "Callas! Callas!" Orleans Street was a little wider than the streets which we had just traversed, and the houses stood shoulder to shoulder, each one with balconies of ornate ironwork which repeated themselves in shadows against the gray brick walls. ... The passage into which we had come was fully fifty feet long and perhaps fifteen feet wide. It was paved with blue-gray flagstones and the long unbroken walls were of mouldering plaster which had been tinted green at some past time, but which were now peeling off in places, showing purplish patches, and here and there a space where bare red bricks could be seen. The ceiling was high above my head and was crossed at intervals by large beams. At the end of the passage, seen through an arch of masonry, was a large courtyard in which bamboo was growing and where tall palm-trees waved in the sunlight. The court was surrounded by the walls of the house, and a balcony extended around three sides of it at the second floor. There was a fountain in the center with a number of small pots of flowering plants ranged around its brim. A tall white statue stood ghostlike at one end, surrounded by a tangle of vines. ... Across the courtyard, at the back, a narrow flight of stairs rose a full three stories, stopping now and then at small landings, then curving and continuing upward. The railing of the stairs was of faded green, and was twined from bottom to top with a magnificent wisteria vine, covered with purple flowers. The whole court was full of color, but so subdued these colors seemed against the vast gray walls that the whole was as dim as some old print that has mellowed with the years. And near the fountain—I had not seen him at first—sat an old gentleman in black, beside a small breakfast table laid in the open air. The sunlight glimmered on the silver coffee-pot, and upon his crest of white hair, and upon a goblet which stood on the white cloth beside his plate. Upon the edge of the goblet sat a green parakeet, dipping its bill into the water.

THE BLUE DOG

Louisiana artist George Rodrigue rocketed to fame with his 30-year series of "Blue Dog" paintings, all based on a spooky Cajun bedtime story called "Loup-Garou." Many think of him as the city's Warhol. Visit the Royal Street Rodrigue Studio to see the evolution of New Orleans' favorite pup.

1984	First Blue Dog, based on Cajun legend of *loup-garou*
1989	Opens first French Quarter gallery
1992	Absolut Vodka full-page Blue Dog ad in USA Today
1997	Inaugural portrait for Clinton-Gore with Blue Dog
2000	Worldwide Xerox ad campaign uses Blue Dog
2001	Tribute painting for 9/11 with White Dog
2005	Prints raise $2.5 million for Katrina relief fund
2008	Sotheby's auctions Blue Dog for $170,500
2013	George Rodrigue, age 69, passes away on Dec 14

TENNESSEE WILLIAMS

A letter to Donald Windham

The Pontchartrain Apartment Hotel
New Orleans, La.
December 26, 1945

Dear Don:

The lovely wind-instrument just reached me and I want to tell you at once how enchanted I am by it, as you must have known I would be. In spite of its extreme fragility it arrived altogether intact, not a bit displaced or broken, and I have been wandering around my room with it, unable to set it down, as it tinkles and jingles. It will go in the brightest spot of my new Apartment which I move into tonight or tomorrow and which is a dream, all the windows being shuttered doors twelve feet high and with a balcony looking out on the negro convent and the back of St. Louis cathedral, easy sanctuary in times of duress. …

I was going home for Xmas but fortunately all north-bound planes were grounded, which heaven-sent dispensation kept me here. Christmas day was one of those exquisitely soft balmy days that occur here between the rains in winter, felt like an angel's kiss. I spent it in the Quarter in the apartment I am going to occupy as the present tenant, moving out this week, was almost as fortuitous a discovery as the apartment itself. It was so warm that we had dinner in a patio and wore skivvy shirts and dungarees. This present tenant has an aged grandmother who is the all-time high in southern ladies innocence. She entered our room this morning at a very early and most inopportune moment and as she strolled by the bed she remarked, "You boys must be cold, I am going to shut these doors."

… My coffee has come up and I must get to work, though it is hard to take my eyes off the wind-instrument. . .

Best wishes for the New Year, and love,

Tennessee

HURRICANE KATRINA

Wreaking havoc in late August and early September of 2005,
Katrina was the costliest hurricane in U.S. history [$161 billion]
and the deadliest [1,836] since 1928.

Aug 24	Tropical Depression 12 strengthens, named Katrina
Aug 26	Pathway changed from FL Panhandle to MS/LA coastline Governor Blanco declares Louisiana state of emergency
Aug 27	At 5 a.m., Katrina reaches Category 3 status Mayor Ray Nagin calls for voluntary evacuation, 5 p.m.
Aug 28	At 7 a.m., winds of 175 mph put storm at Category 5 Mandatory evacuation of Orleans Parish Superdome opened as "refuge of last resort" for 30,000
Aug 29	Eye of hurricane passes over city Levee breaches at 17th Street and Industrial canals Power goes out at Superdome Ninth Ward under 8-10 feet of water
Aug 30	Superdome ordered to be evacuated, takes 5 days
Aug 31	80 percent of city underwater, 53 levee breaches Infamous Air Force One photograph of President Bush Memorial Medical Center—no power, no water, 100 degrees
Sep 1	Bridge into Gretna blocked by armed police officers FEMA's Michael Brown tells CNN "no reports of unrest" Helicopter rescues continue, total up to 4,489 residents
Sep 2	Algiers man, Henry Glover, murdered by NOPD "Brownie, you're doing a heck of a job," Bush to FEMA's Brown
Sep 4	Police shoot two unarmed people on Danziger Bridge
Sep 9	Homeland Security blocks all media access, CNN files lawsuit
Sep 11	45 dead patients recovered from Memorial Medical Center
Sep 12	FEMA's Michael Brown resigns
Sep 15	President Bush delivers speech from Jackson Square
Sep 19	Hurricane Rita on horizon, second evacuation ordered
Oct 13	Over 600,000 refugees living in subsidized hotels
Nov 23	Over 6,500 adults unaccounted for, 400 bodies unidentified

Star Jasmine

Giant Blue Flag

Gardenia

Banana Tree

Agapanthus

Angel's Trumpet

FLORA OF NOTE

Plant name	Description
Chinese Wisteria	*hanging lavender bouquets in April and May*
Dutchman's Pipe	*green tropical climbers known as Pelican plant; invasive*
Star Jasmine	*intoxicating, white-petalled vines overflow like bouffants*
Indigo Spires	*bold blue spikes, tough-minded through first frost*
Bougainvillea	*booming tropical billows with three blooms a year*
Arborvitae Fern	*pale-green, lacy varietal, shady, moist home*
Banana Tree	*red, pink-velvet and classic, bright-green elephant ears*
Agapanthus	*periwinkle fireworks, known as Lily of the Nile*
Giant Blue Flag	*purple-blue iris is official state wildflower of Louisiana*
Wild Sweet William	*early summer blooms, lavender, white and blue*
Gardenia	*lustrous dark foliage, champion white flowers*
Angel's Trumpet	*poisonous, pale purple to white, lemony scent*
Shrimp Plant	*pinkish-red flowers shaped like giant prawns*
Macho Fern	*balcony behemoths can grow six feet in width*
Mamou Plant	*early pop of red, Native tribes used for bowel pain*
Toadshade	*perennial trillium, foul stench from inner flower*
Beautyberry	*metallic sheen on clustered berries, good for jellies*
Sweet Olive	*hints of orange-apricot induce heavenly deep breathing*
Spanish Flag	*red-to-yellow ombré, also called firecracker vine*
Honeybush	*sweet, sugary smell with leaves ready for tea steeping*

MARDI GRAS INDIANS

A list of traditional Black Masking Tribes, past and present.

Apache Hunters

Black Eagles

Blackfoot Hunters

Black Hawk Hunters

Carrollton Hunters

Cheyenne Hunters

Comanche Hunters

Creole Osceola

Creole Wild West

Diamond Stars

Eastern Cherokee

Eight Bad Men

Fi Yi Yi

Flaming Arrows

Geronimo Hunters

Golden Arrows

Golden Blades

Golden Eagles

Golden Sioux

Golden Star Hunters

Guardians of the Flame

Mohawk Hunters

Morning Star Hunters

Ninth Ward Hunters

Original Yellow Jackets

Red Flame Hunters

Red, White and Blue

Second Ward Hunters

Seminole Warriors

Seventh Ward Hunters

Shabbe Hunters

Hundred and One

Third Ward Terrors

Trouble Nation

White Cloud Hunters

White Eagles

Wild Apache

Wild Bogocheetus

Wild Magnolias

Wild Squatoulas

Wild Tchoupitoulas

Yellow Jackets

Yellow Pocahontas

Young Brave Hunters

NOTABLE KREWES

Mistick Krewe of Comus	*In 1991, New Orleans passed an ordinance that required krewes to open their doors to all, regardless of race or gender. Historic Comus, along with Momus and Proteus, withdrew from parading rather than comply.......1856*
Krewe of Rex	*Formed as city recovered from the Civil War, they are originators of the official Carnival colors of purple, green and gold.......1872*
Zulu Social Aid & Pleasure Club	*Predominantly Black krewe, whose king first paraded wearing a lard-can crown and banana-stalk scepter to parody white Mardi Gras. Throw hand-decorated "golden nugget" coconuts.......1909*
Krewe of Endymion	*One of the "super krewes," defined by stunning visuals and technology. In 2013, they set a world record for the largest Mardi Gras float—330 feet long, 230 riders, $1.2 million to build.......1967*
Mystic Krewe of Barkus	*All dogs dressed up in costume.......1992*
Krewe du Jieux	*Krewe of Jews and the "Jew-ish" aiming to draw attention to the absurdity of Jews being historically excluded from Mardi Gras celebrations in New Orleans. Throw hand-decorated bagels.......1996*
Krewe of Muses	*All-women krewe that throws elaborately hand-decorated shoes.......2000*
'tit Rəx	*Instead of massive floats that take up entire blocks, theirs are tiny, made out of shoe boxes pulled on strings.......2009*

"POSEIDON, KING OF SEA, RULES OVER HOLMES BALL WITH MISS MCCABE QUEEN"

Times-Picayune
February 7, 1927

POSEIDON, King of the Sea, held sway with his queen over revelers at the D. H. Holmes Carnival ball last night in the Athaneum. The large ballroom was decorated to represent the meeting of the waves and the sky, the realms of Poseidon and of mortals, the tableaux carrying out the theme in attractive, colorful display. Poseidon was represented by Paul Bailey, the popularly chosen king, his queen being Miss Myrtle McCabe, whose royalty also was declared by acclamation. At 9 o'clock, the curtain rose upon the first tableaux of the Carnival pageant, a scene representing the ocean, bathing girls and a ballet and titled "Moonlight and the Waves." The ballet, presented by Miss Jeanne Ploger, caught the spirit of dancing waves and glittering moonlight and merged them into one. The second curtain rose on "The Rainbow Trail," an intricate figure presented by the Cotillion Club of eighty young women and twenty men. Ballet costumes of pastel rainbow hues and harlequins in the same lovely colorings came from right and left wings of the stage to form entrancing figures on the stage and then, a circle on the ballroom floor. Following the tableaux of the sea, Poseidon and his court were shown awaiting the queen and maids. Their arrival, announced by a royal bugler before the footlights, brought a crescendo of applause and preceded the grand march of the royal party and the maskers. The queen gowned in white and silver, with rhinestones and pearls for jewels, was a fitting complement to the green-mantled glory of Poseidon and his jewels of rhinestones and emeralds. Following the grand march, E. Davis McCutchon, captain, led the march of the maskers.

RUBY BRIDGES

Escorted by four U.S. Marshals, six-year-old Ruby Bridges walked through the doors of a New Orleans elementary school on November 14, 1960 and, with her small steps, was the first student to desegregate the city's public schools. Below, an article from Alexandria, Louisiana's The Town Talk *detailing the scene after efforts to defy the decision from* Brown v. Board of Education *failed.*

The ruling enraged the cursing "cheerleaders" as the police call some 40 women who haunt the William Frantz school area to jeer and poke at white parents who break a white student boycott. One Negro girl attends Frantz. … The "cheerleaders" were held back by police when they tried to attack a white mother, Mrs. Daisy Gabrielle, whose first-grade daughter Yolanda attends the school but sits in a separate room from Ruby Bridges, the lone first grade Negro girl. One of the irate women did manage to reach past police and shove Mrs. Gabrielle against a tree. Mrs. Gabrielle, who served in WACS in World War II rebounded and when the "cheerleader" wound up on the ground, a policeman looked down and said, "You shoved first."

One of Norman Rockwell's more recognizable and political works, "The Problem We All Live With," depicts Bridges walking into school behind the legs of the U.S. Marshals, with watery streaks of tomatoes thrown against the wall of the school in the background.

STREET NAMES

Visitors to New Orleans are often baffled by the street names' pronunciations, but a section in the city's Lower Garden District named for the Muses proves most confusing. Creole architect, city planner and sometimes-pirate Barthélemy Lafon named them during his tenure as an Orleans Parish surveyor. Below, a list of the mythology-influenced streets.

CALLIOPE: kal-ee-OPE

CLIO: CLEE-oh or C-L-ten

ERATO: EAR-rah-toe

THALIA: THAIL-ya

MELPOMENE: MEL-po-meen

TERPSICHORE: TURP-sah-cree or TURP-sah-core

EUTERPE: YOU-turp

POLYMNIA: PAH-lem-nee-ya

URANIA: YUR-rain-ya

A LETTER FROM LOUIS ARMSTRONG

Evansville Ind.
September 25th, 1942,

I've done things a lot of times
And I've done them in a Hustle
But I break my neack [sic] almost every time
To write to my boy-Wm Russell,..
Lawd Today.

'How'Doo' Brother Russell:

Man—you talking about a 'Cat thaw, been trying his 'damnedest to get this fine chance to write to you my friend it was'Mee....My'Gawd....I never thought that one man could be as busy as your boy Ol Satchmo Gatemouth! Louis Armstrong....ha....ha....But 'Ah'Wuz'....ha....You talk about a guy being as busy as a one arm paper hanger with 'crabs...tee her—Dats Mee....But I was just determined to let you hear from me'Gate....

I also want to thank you for being so kind as to send me one of those fine books of yours, "Jazzmen"....I've 'Scanned the ass off it already—and it's a Solid Sender....Honest. It's undoubtedly the best book on Jazz-yet....Theres none other that can 'Cut It in my estimation....You really tells the folks what it's all about when it comes to really taking about New Orleans LA....Yessir Mr Russell your book tells about New Orleans just the way I [personally] saw it when New Orleans was a New Orleans....'Yarsuh....Of course it's just the 'Remnants now....tee her....

Well Brother Russ, I'll have to do you like the Farmer did the Potatoe, I'll plant ya now-and 'Dig ya later....tee her....So take me slow and tell all of the Fans that ol Satchmo said to take it easy....Also tell them—by the time you get this letter I'll have my Divorce from my third wife and I'll be on my way to the Altar with my fourth wife....Which is the sharpest one of all of them. Yessir—Madam Lucille Wilson is gonna make all of the rest of the Mrs Satchmo's look sick when she walks down the Aisle with Brother Satchmo Armstrong looking just too-pretty for words with her little Brown

Cute Self....Lawd today....

Here's saying goodnight and God Bless you brother Russell...And if Lucille and I have more than one Satchmo—I'll name one of them Russell....Your Name....Nice?....You see the first one will have to be named Satchmo Louis Armstrong Jr... Savy?....ha... And believe me Pal—we're really going to get down to real—'Biz'nez this time. Catch on?—Oh Boy...

Am Redbeans and Ricely Yours,

[Signature] Louis Armstrong

SUPERSTITION AND LORE

Always burn the onion peels and you will always have money.

....

To hurt an enemy, put his name in a dead bird's mouth and let the bird dry up.

....

If someone has bitten you, put some chicken manure on the wound and all your enemy's teeth will fall out.

....

To make the chicken stay home, spit in its throat and throw it up the chimney.

....

To get rid of a man, pick a rooster naked, give him a spoonful of whiskey, then put in his beak a piece of paper on which is written nine times the name of the person to be gotten rid of. Turn the rooster loose in St. Roch's cemetery. Within three days the man will die.

....

To drive a woman crazy, sprinkle nutmeg in her left shoe every night at midnight.

> *These superstitions were gathered by Louisiana writer Robert Tallant, who participated in the WPA Writers' Project in the 1930s.*

THANKING THE SAINTS

*Published in the "Personal" advertisements section
of the* Times-Picayune, *April* 1928.

THANKS to Sacred Heart of Jesus for favor granted. Mrs. T. O'Neil

THANKS to St. Jude for favor granted. Holy masses and publication promised. A Client.

THANKS to the Sacred Heart of Jesus, His Immaculate Mother, St. Joseph, and St. Anthony for favors granted. Mrs. C.

THANKS to St. Rita and Little Flower of Jesus for special favor granted. Mrs. Charles H. Frantz, 920 Jena.

THANKS to the Little Theresa, Flower of Jesus and St. Jude. N. N. M.

THANKS to St. Michael the archangel, Our Lady of Prompt Succor, My Guardian Angel, my two little angels in heaven, Willie and Regina, also to Father Pro, the Mexican martyred priest for extraordinary favors granted me. W. T. L.

AM applying for a pardon or commutation of sentence. *JOHN LIGHTFOOT.*

NOT responsible for debts contorted by my wife, George G. Moll.

THANKS to St. Anthony for finding silver. Promised publication. M. B. V.

PROMISED PUBLICATION. Thanks to Our Lady of Prompt Succor for saving city from flood last May. M. B. V.

ED—Am trying to make Tuesday as usual. Clara.

I AM NOT responsible for any debts contorted by my wife. STEVE CESKA.

ANY member of Col. Dreure's Orleans Guards during Civil war remembering Charles L. F. Platz, please phone his widow. Uptown 2176-W.

THANKS to St. Januarius and Companions for favor. Mrs. L. H.

THANKS to St. Theresa, Little Flower of Jesus, for safe return of my dog. Mrs. F. F. P.

THE DEAD VOUDOU QUEEN
Marie Laveau's Place in the History of New-Orleans

The New York Times
June 23, 1881

NEW-ORLEANS. — Marie Laveau, the "Queen of the Voudous" died last Wednesday at the advanced age of 98 years. To the superstitious creoles Marie appeared as a dealer in the black arts and a person to be dreaded and avoided. Strange stories were told of the rites performed by the sect of which Marie was the acknowledged sovereign. Many old residents asserted that on St. John's night, the 24th of June, the Voudou clan had been seen in deserted places joining in wild, weird dances, all the participants in which were perfectly nude. The Voudous were thought to be invested with supernatural powers, and men sought them to find means to be rid of their enemies, while others asked for love powders to instill affection into the bosoms of their unwilling or unsuspecting sweethearts. Whether there ever was any such sect, and whether Marie was ever its Queen, her life was one to render such a belief possible. Besides knowing the secret healing qualities of the various herbs which grew in abundance in the woods and fields, she was endowed with more than the usual share of common sense, and her advice was oft-times really valuable and her penetration remarkable. Adding to these qualities the gift of great beauty, no wonder that she possessed a large influence in her youth and attracted the attention of Louisiana's greatest men and most distinguished visitors. In [the Laveau mansion] Marie received the celebrities of the day. Lawyers, legislators, planters, merchants, all came to pay their respects to her and seek her offices, and the narrow room heard as much wit and scandal as any of the historical *salons* of Paris. There were business men who would not send a ship to sea before consulting her upon the probabilities of the voyage.

BETSY SURVIVOR RELATES HORROR OF NEW ORLEANS FLOOD DISASTER

September 13, 1965

NEW ORLEANS, La. [AP]—Willie Brown had returned to his home on Reynes Street last Thursday night and was relaxing in an easy chair.

For the last 20 years, Willie has been a chef at a restaurant across from Charity Hospital. He's a round little man of 50 who wears glasses and moves at an easy gait because of heart trouble.

He's unathletic looking and can't swim.

"Sure I was worried about Betsy but I had been through hurricanes before," he said. "I figured I could go through another one."

As Willie remembers, it was about 9:30 p.m. when he put his glasses and wallet on top of this television set and dozed off.

"I didn't have any juice [electricity] so I had no TV," he said. "I had no trouble falling asleep."

Willie might have spent all night in his chair—except he was suddenly awakened an hour later.

"I felt something cold, looked down and there I was with water in my lap," he said.

"I jumped out of the chair, raced to the back door and opened it. Swoosh! In came the water. It had me around the shoulder and, for a moment, I was about to go crazy.

"All I could think of was me and Lady—that's my dog. I grabbed Lady and I really can't tell you how but I climbed up an iron railing and made it on top of my roof."

Willie figures the top part of his roof is about 15 feet high.

"By the time I got up there," he says, "the water was lapping at my pants and the wind was pouring in all around. It was all I could do to keep Lady under my arm and put my fingernails into the tar paper.

"Three times during the night I was blown off and I had to claw my way back up to the top."

Willie Brown's battle for life lasted 19 hours—ending at 5:30 p.m. Friday when a motorboat plucked him and several of his neighbors from their rooftop refuge.

"God it was like one big swimming pool as far as the eye could see," says Willie. "There were people I knew, women, children, screaming and praying."

The night of terror as Betsy was whipping through with 120 miles an hour winds was bad enough. But even though the wind had abated, daylight brought a picture forever etched in Willie Brown's memory.

"It must have been around eight in the morning when a lady who lives down the block floated past, with her two children right alongside. I guess the wind was too much or I guess she just gave out."

Along with the bodies were a number of deadly water snakes and every time he saw one Willie's fingers dug deeper in the tar paper.

"I guess you can say I lost everything but my life," says Willie. "But that makes me a lot luckier than a lot of folks. You can always get some clothes and earn money to buy food and find a place to stay. So I sure can't complain. You have thousands a lot worse off than me."

COOKBOOKS

THE PICAYUNE'S CREOLE COOK BOOK
Fascinating to see how [little] things change, 1900

RIVER ROAD RECIPES
Dog-eared Baton Rouge home-cook series, 1959

THE NEW ORLEANS RESTAURANT COOKBOOK
The institutions: Commander's, Arnaud's, more, 1967

CREOLE FEAST
Black master chefs share the classics, 1978

LOUISIANA KITCHEN
Chef Paul Prudhomme puts Cajun spice on the map, 1984

THE LITTLE GUMBO BOOK
More than two dozen ways to roux, 1986

THE DOOKY CHASE COOKBOOK
Leah Chase's soulful story and recipes, 1990

GALATOIRE'S COOKBOOK
Delicious recipe secrets spilled, more than 140 in all, 2005

REAL CAJUN
Donald Link's Beard Award-winner, 2009

MOSQUITO SUPPER CLUB
Melissa Martin's ode to modern Cajun cooking and her fishing-village home, 2020

HANSEN'S SNO-BLIZ

*Opened in 1934, Hansen's is the king of New Orleans sno-balls—
homemade syrups generously drizzled over velvety ice. Not much has
changed on Tchoupitoulas, including the patented ice shaver designed and
built by founder Ernest Hansen.*

U.S. PATENT 707,364
NOVEMBER 2, 1946

The present invention relates to new and useful improvements in ice shaving machines and more particularly to a power operated machine of this character including a rotary cutter for shaving a block of ice into substantially fine particles.

An important object of the invention is to provide a machine of this character including a manually operated follower for feeding the block of ice in a step by step movement toward the cutter.

An additional object of the invention is to provide a manually operated pressure plate for holding the block of ice against movement while being shaved and by means of which pressure is being maintained on the block of ice while being fed toward the cutter.

....

1. An ice shaving machine comprising a casing, an ice chamber in said casing, a rotary cutter journalled at one end of the chamber, a discharge spout leading from said end, a follower member in said chamber for advancing a block of ice longitudinally therein, an operating bar extending from said member, means for engaging the bar and moving the follower member toward the cutter, a plate hingedly mounted in the ice chamber for holding the block of ice against lateral movement, means for urging the plate from contact with the ice block, and means for moving and holding said plate in contact with the ice, said last means including a rod extending from said plate, an operating bar seated on said rod, a foot pedal, and flexible connecting means between said bar downwardly upon actuation of the pedal.

UPSTAIRS LOUNGE FIRE

> ## 29 DEAD IN QUARTER HOLOCAUST
>
> "13 Fire Victims are Identified"

The States-Item Flash
June 23, 1973

POLICE today tentatively identified 13 of 29 persons killed by the worst fire in the modern history of New Orleans.

The long process of trying to identify what was left after a fast-moving, 16-minute inferno left bodies stacked like pancakes in a French Quarter bar was assigned to a Charity Hospital team today.

Tentatively identified as victims of the fire, without addresses, are Leon Maples, Louis Broussard, John Goldring, Donald Dunbar, George Mitchell, Clarence McCloskey, Inez Warren, Joe Bailey, Guy Anderson, David S. Gary, Norman Lavergne, Kenneth Harrington and Jerry Gordon.

"We don't even know if these papers belonged to the people we found them on," Morris said. "Some thieves hung out there and you know this was a queer bar." Another police source said it is not uncommon for homosexuals to carry false identification, which could complicate the identification procedure.

Twenty-eight of the 29 killed were men and the place was packed for the weekly Sunday night beer bust, a kind of happy hour featuring all you could eat and drink for $2.

About 20 men were led to safety through a rear exit by a bartender, through a kind of theater and down a little-known fire escape.

Courtney Craighead, a survivor of the blaze, said he believes somebody dashed an inflammable liquid on the stairway and lit it. "The fire came up so fast," he said. "There was an immense smoke in the room immediately."

William White, 18, of Pineville, said he and Gary Williams, 19, also of Pineville, wandered into the bar while nosing around in the French Quarter. He said they might have stayed except for a bit of luck.

"There was a couple of guys quarreling at the top of the stairs," White said. "I don't like no kind of fights so we left. We weren't more than a block away when I looked back—the whole place was lit up by fire."

CONGO SQUARE

In 1724, the French government issued 54 articles governing social inter-action between whites, enslaved people, and free people of color of Loui-siana. The harsh edicts of "Le Code Noir" remained law of the land until 1803, but one of its rules planted the seed for the creation of jazz. Article V stated: "Sundays and holidays are to be strictly observed. All negroes found at work on these days are to be confiscated." With labor-free Sundays, enslaved people would gather to sell goods, dance and perform music at what today is called Congo Square, a small plaza in the Tremé neighborhood. The play-ing of African rhythms on new soil synthesized the beats and improvisation that would give rise to the distinctly American art form, jazz. According to Wynton Marsalis, "The bloodlines of all important modern American mu-sic can be traced to Congo Square." The nonprofit arts and culture publica-tion *64 Parishes* also notes the legally tenuous nature of these weekly gather-ings: "The rhythms and variations played in Congo Square are found at the core of early New Orleans jazz compositions and became an integral part of indigenous New Orleans music. They are still heard in second line and parade beats, the music and songs of Mardi Gras Indians, and the music of brass bands that play for jazz funerals and black social aid and pleasure club parades. … No law, however, granted enslaved people the right to congregate, and the privilege for them to do so was constantly under threat. Any effort or rumor of an effort to revolt and gain real freedom jeopardized their ability to come together. Yet, from the earliest days of the colony, under different laws and conditions, Africans gathered at every opportunity. They congregated discontinuously at various locations in the city—along levees, in backyards, on plantations, in remote areas, and in other public squares on Sunday af-ternoons, until 1817. That year a city ordinance restricted all assemblies of the enslaved for the purposes of dancing and merriment to one location ap-pointed by the mayor. The designated place was Congo Square."

The story of New Orleans is inseparable from America's history of slavery. Researchers estimate that over 100,000 enslaved Africans, nearly a third children, were auctioned in pre-Civil War New Orleans. The everyday realities for enslaved people were absolute horror, and the legacy of the practice is directly tied to the complex difficulties of modern-day New Orleans—the failures of Katrina, prison populations, public housing and more. To learn more, visit Tulane University's Amistad Research Center.

THE SECOND LINE

New Orleans Jazz Club
July & August, 1950

To the Editor:

I want to tell you a true story. One hot, muggy night in June, 1902, a group of us, all boys, from the Hospital St. and Chartres St. section of New Orleans silently crept toward the rear of Saia's Stableyard but we bumped smack into the big smokestack of Seidel's furniture factory!

However, we finally found, via the moonlight, an empty stall, and we quickly arranged the washboards and tin cans and old zinc tubs.... Then the two harmonica wizards of the 90's let loose with what we called "Cheer Up Mary". Poor old Mary surely got a dressing up that evening!

But something must have happened to Lula, the mule in the nearest stall, because as soon as we started playing Lula gave a wild snort and leaped clear over the chain bar. Meanwhile, from the chicken roost to the right of our newly acquired jam parlor, came a flutter of wings in all directions. Some of the chickens flew up on the shed, while some scattered over fences and finally into the street but the Tin Pan Serenaders never stopped playing. The two boys on harmonica were "Mexican" Piet and "Chinese" Pauly, respectively, and they were GOOD!!

The inimitable rhythm of the washboard, the tin kettle and the big zinc tub sounded like the coming of Jehova! All we needed was a long trumpet, and Moses could have added another commandment to the other ten. The noise was terrific. I still remember the big, leaky washtub before me. It's incredible, but our time was perfect; that 4/4 beat of later days never varied. ... Then came a barrage of old shoes, potatoes, watermelon rinds, finally a brick! We promptly retreated.

The quickest way out of the yard was over the back fence to Seidel's lumber yard, and out to Barracks St. Thus ended the first Jam Session of the Tin Pan Serenaders, later on the Regal Orchestra!

This group of 1902 grew and months later included Tom Early, Herbert Decueirs, Joe Pollizzi, Chink Martin, Alex Sposito, Bull Riley, Frank Otero, Wing Mazzarini, and myself. I doubled on cornet with Johnny Lala, in the Regal Orchestra. Emanuel Allessandro was on clarinet but he 'turned' classical soon after. Tots Blaise replaced Mazzarini on drums; Chink Martin joined Papa Laine's band and was replaced by Paul Venerella on bass fiddle. The late Leon Mello who stepped into Bull Riley's shoes was one of the best 'fake' trombonists, anywhere. He played on the order of our present George Brunis.

Without shaking peaches from anybody's tree, the famous Regal Orchestra, which had its inception in Saia's Stable in June 1902, and which later appeared in Quarella's Pavillion, in Milneburg, took no water from any other Jazz outfit of that period!!

Today, almost fifty years later, history doesn't know a single member of this group who struggled relentlessly to bring Jazz to the world!

Over-night critics and pseudo-historians who don't know a cornet from a bottleman's horn are the sole cause of this. Had we men and women to defend us like the fine group we have today in the New Orleans Jazz Club, the history of authentic Jazz of the 90's would be well known. A few of us still remain, the original jazzmen of the old guard. These musicians will always have a soft spot in their inner hearts for the New Orleans Jazz Club.

As their messenger, I say THANKS.

Johnny Provenzano,

1450 N. Villere St.,
New Orleans, La.

On February 21, 1948, a small, devoted group of jazz aficionados launched the New Orleans Jazz Club. Two years later, they began publishing a monthly bulletin, called The Second Line, *typed-up with smart commentary, the latest jazz news and unabashed affection for the masters. For more, visit nojazzclub.org or the Hogan Jazz Archive on Tulane's campus.*

RIVER COMMERCE

All commodities shipped along the Mississippi, from Baton Rouge, mile 236, to Mouth of Passes, mile 0, in 2012. Measured in short tons.

TOTAL COMMODITIES	456,550,669
Coal, Lignite, Coal Coke	61,855,767
Crude Petroleum	32,250,276
Gasoline	17,265,668
Fuel Oil, Distillate/Residual	67,293,219
Fertilizers	20,875,854
Other Chemicals	31,722,381
Radioactive Materials	12,003
Forest Products, Rubber, Chips, Lumber	591,897
Soil, Sand, Gravel, Rock, Stone	15,105,671
Iron Ore and Scrap	8,084,658
Paper Products, Newsprint	242,905
Lime, Cement, Glass	2,279,104
Wheat, Corn, Grains	54,410,971
Peanuts, Soybeans, Flaxseeds, Oilseeds	62,124,846
Meat, Fresh and Frozen	352,969
Sugar	721,190
Coffee	264,080
Dairy Products	103
Alcoholic Beverages	105,956
Machinery and Equipment	1,660,139
Waste, Garbage, Sewage Sludge, Landfill, Waste Water	192,895

THE AINTS

Long before the "Who Dat" heroics of 2010, the New Orleans Saints were bottom-dwellers of the National Football League. The lowest point came in 1980, when 0-12, fans attended a home game wearing brown paper sacks over their heads. Not even star quarterback Archie Manning could save the "Aints" from a historically disastrous season.

Week	Opponent	Result
1	San Francisco 49ers	L, 23-26
2	Chicago Bears	L, 3-22
3	Buffalo Bills	L, 26-35
4	Miami Dolphins	L, 16-21
5	St. Louis Cardinals	L, 7-40
6	Detroit Lions	L, 13-24
7	Atlanta Falcons	L, 14-41
8	Washington Redskins	L, 14-22
9	Los Angeles Rams	L, 31-45
10	Philadelphia Eagles	L, 21-34
11	Atlanta Falcons	L, 13-31
12	Los Angeles Rams	L, 7-27
13	Minnesota Vikings	L, 20-23
14	San Francisco 49ers	L, 35-38
15	New York Jets	W, 21-20
16	New England Patriots	L, 27-38

NICKNAMES

- Nouvelle Orleans
- Nueva Orleans
- Great Southern Babylon
- Wet Grave
- Necropolis of the South
- Crescent City
- Queen of the South
- City that Care Forgot
- The Big Easy
- Chocolate City
- Hollywood South
- Who Dat Nation

BIRDS OF NOTE

Species	Appearance.........Habitat
Brown Pelican	Long, flat bill for plunge-fishing...beaches and boat docks
Black Skimmer	Tuxedo look, cute underbite...sandbars, shallow inlets and estuaries
Roseate Spoonbill	Inspired shades of pink, "flame birds"...gregariously gathered in lakes and spillways
Clapper Rail	Rusty plumage, skinny bill...salt marshes, listen for summer rattling kek-kek
Little Blue Heron	Solemn gray coat, black-tipped bill...freshwater swamps or insect hunting behind tractors
Red Knot	Pinkish coloring, size of a robin...winters on shallow coastlines
Great Egret	Snow white, bright lores around eyes...clogged cypress swamp rookeries
Glossy Ibis	Basic black-brown, though breeders have green shine...wetland generalist

BOUNCE

New Orleans' brand of hip-hop combines chant-style shoutouts, a "Trigger-man beat" and energetic call and response. Most critics agree that 1991's "Where Dey At" launched the genre. Below, a list of bounce artists.

Soulja Slim	U.N.L.V.	Choppa
Big Freedia	Katey Red	10th Ward Buck
Juvenile	Nicky Da B	Baby Erin
Magnolia Shorty	Partners-N-Crime	Magnolia Rhome
Silky Slim	Kane & Abel	Flipset Fred
Elm Boy Peg	Calliope Ceedy	Sissy Nobby
5th Ward Weebie	Cheeky Blakk	MC T. Tucker
Keezy Kilo	Lady Unique	DJ Duck
Lil Wayne	Jo Jackson	DJ Money Fresh

PLESSY V. FERGUSON

One man taking a seat on a New Orleans streetcar led to this landmark 1896 Supreme Court ruling. Often declared one of the worst judicial decisions in American history, it upheld the constitutionality of racial segregation and the "separate but equal" doctrine. Homer Plessy, a free person of color and member of the Comité des Citoyens, a local civil rights group devoted to Black empowerment, refused to move from the "whites-only" streetcar as a committee-orchestrated act to protest segregation. An 1892 article from The Crusader, *a newspaper that often published the work of the group's founder Rodolphe Lucien Desdunes, describes the mission.*

He held a first-class ticket and naturally took his seat in a first-class coach. As the train was moving out of the station, the conductor came up and asked him if he was a white man. Plessy, who is as white as the average white Southerner, replied that he was a colored man. Then, said the conductor, "you must go in the coach reserved for colored people." Plessy replied that he had a first-class ticket and would remain in the first-class coach. The conductor insisted that he retire to the Jim Crow coach. Plessy determinedly told him that he was an American citizen and proposed to enjoy his rights as such and to ride for the value of his money. The conductor, seeing his own powers of persuasion unavailing, invoked the aid of the police. Capt. C.C. Cain, who was at the station, entered the car and told Plessy that if he was a colored man he would have to go to the colored coach. Plessy again refused. The officer told him he would have to go into the coach or to jail. Plessy said he would go to jail first before relinquishing his right as a citizen. The conductor signaled the engineer, and the train, which was moving slowly, came to a stand still at the intersection of Rampart street, and the officer alighted with Plessy and a couple of citizens, who apparently had volunteered their aid to make the arrest. Plessy was conducted to the Fifth precinct station, where a charge for violating the separate car law was booked against him. By this time a few friends of Plessy—Messrs. Eugene Luscy, Paul Bonseigneur, R.L. Desdune, L.J. Joubert and L.A. Martinet—hearing of his arrest, had repaired to the station. They called on Judge Moulin who kindly let him out on temporary bail, to appear the next day at the Second Recorder's Court. ...The Citizens' Committee will seek to have invalidated the Jim Crow car law as applying to local passengers also—passengers from one point to another point in the State; it will seek to establish the right of the citizen to travel interstate and intrastate unmolested and without danger of LEGAL affront or indignity.

GALATOIRE'S

No other American city can claim as many centuries-old restaurants still in action as New Orleans, from Antoine's, founded in 1840, to Tujague's, in 1856. One of the French Quarter's longest-running restaurants, Galatoire's remains a favorite for long, rambling Friday lunches. Below, items listed on a menu from approximately 1950.

....

NOTHING SERVED LESS THAN 25 CENTS PER PERSON

TABLE D'HÔTE DINNER FROM 5 TO 9, $1.00,
WITH SMALL BOTTLE WINE, $1.25

MERCHANTS' LUNCH FROM 11 TO 2, 70 CENTS

NOT RESPONSIBLE FOR LOST ARTICLES

OYSTERS [When in Season]

Raw, on Half Shell

Stew, in Milk

Stew, in Cream

Fried

Broiled, or en Brochette

Fried in Butter

Scalloped or Pan Roast

Patties

À la Créole

Rockefeller

Poulette

SOUPS

Consommé

Vermicelli

Turtle

Oyster

Gumbo

Créole Gumbo

Cream of Tomato

Bisque [When in Season]

FISH, SHRIMP and CRABS

Trout Marguery

Fish en Papillote

Broiled Pompano

Trout Meunière

Tenderloin of Trout,
Tartare Sauce

Broiled Sheepshead,
Hollandaise Sauce

Red Fish, Courtbouillon
with Rice

River Shrimp, Iced

Lake Shrimp, Iced

Lake Shrimp Remoulade

Crab Meat Cocktail

Crab Meat Au Gratin

Stuffed Crab

Iced Crayfish

Frog Legs, Tartare Sauce

Soft Shell Crab [2]

Busters, Broiled or Fried

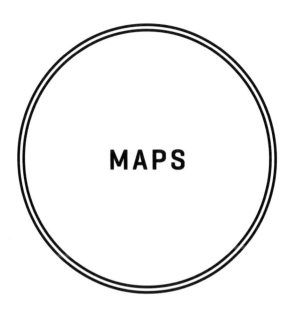

MAPS

Pictorial journeys through unique New Orleans
culture, commerce and landscapes by local
illustrator Scott Campbell. Not to scale.

CLASSIC CUISINE

★

LIUZZA'S BY
THE TRACK

★

CAFÉ DU MONDE
AT CITY PARK

★ PARKWAY
BAKERY

COMMANDER'S
PALACE

★

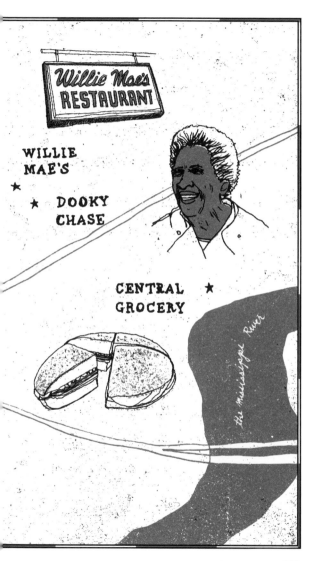

WILLIE MAE'S

DOOKY CHASE

CENTRAL GROCERY

the mississippi River

CLASSIC CUISINE

The best examples of the New Orleans culinary canon can be found all over the city, from corner dives to white-tablecloth temples.

GUMBO
LIUZZA'S BY THE TRACK
A very dark roux layered with seafood, locally made sausage, okra and 13 seasonings. During springtime's Jazz Fest, this spot becomes a port in the storm, figuratively and literally. *1518 N Lopez St*

SEAFOOD PO'BOY
PARKWAY BAKERY AND TAVERN
This century-old joint on the bayou builds its po'boys tall. The move: a fried Gulf shrimp "dressed" with a bag of crunchy Zapp's Cajun Crawtator chips and an ice-cold bottle of Barq's root beer. *538 Hagen Ave*

TURTLE SOUP
COMMANDER'S PALACE
Once the dish in vogue in early America. Commander's still makes it with real turtle meat, spinach and hard-boiled eggs. Don't decline the tableside drizzle of sherry. *1403 Washington Ave*

FRIED CHICKEN
WILLIE MAE'S SCOTCH HOUSE
Fried-to-order, the chicken at this Tremé cornerstone comes with a shatteringly crunchy crust. *2401 St Ann St*

BEIGNETS
CAFÉ DU MONDE
But don't line up at the French Quarter original. Instead, walk right up to the order window at its pretty, patioed outpost in City Park. *56 Dreyfous Dr*

MUFFULETTA
CENTRAL GROCERY & DELI
Layered with ham, salami, cheese and marinated-olive salad on a Leidenheimer bun. This is the sandwich's origin. *923 Decatur St*

RED BEANS & RICE
DOOKY CHASE'S RESTAURANT
Leah Chase's family continues to stir the iconic chef's pots of gumbo z'herbes, red beans and shrimp creole. *2301 Orleans Ave*

MORE CLASSICS *Fried oysters at Upperline; roast beef po'boy at Parasol's; duck and dirty rice at Brigtsen's; creole eggplant at Mandina's; BBQ shrimp pie at Gabrielle.*

MARDI GRAS

In this town, Mardi Gras is only one day of a weeks-long party. Here, seven Carnival-season landmarks.

MARDI GRAS WORLD

Founder Blaine Kern created the city's modern parade float aesthetic for super krewes Orpheus, Bacchus and Endymion. Working warehouse studio offers tours. *1380 Port of New Orleans Pl*

BROADWAY BOUND COSTUMES

Feathers, sequins, marabou, jewels and glitter by the pound. All the sparkle, flash and color you need to make a few weeks' worth of costumes. *2737 Canal St*

CLAIBORNE UNDERPASS

A barrier bisecting a community reclaimed as a gathering space. Brass bands, Mardi Gras Indian marches and second lines all echo inside this tunnel of sound during Carnival.

FIFI MAHONY'S

French Quarter wig shop specializing in custom hairpieces for Mardi Gras, from Marie Antoinettes to bouffants. Bywater location's hair salon specializes in flamboyant color treatments. *934 Royal St*

CRESCENT CITY STEAKS

Crammed on Mardi Gras Day, as it's a favored spot for the last beef many people eat before Lent. *1001 N Broad St*

R BAR

Primo viewing spot on Mardi Gras morning for the decidedly informal Bywater- and Marigny-based St. Anne Parade, where marchers model an endless array of elaborate handmade costumes. *1431 Royal St*

ROYAL SONESTA

Hosts annual Greasing of the Poles with Vaseline to prevent revelers from climbing up the poles to the hotel's balcony. Celebrity greasers compete for prizes from a panel of judges. *300 Bourbon St*

COCONUT CONUNDRUM *In 1988, Louisiana's legislature passed SB188, the "Coconut Bill," which excluded the Krewe of Zulu's coconuts, one of Mardi Gras' most prized throws, from liability lawsuits due to injury.*

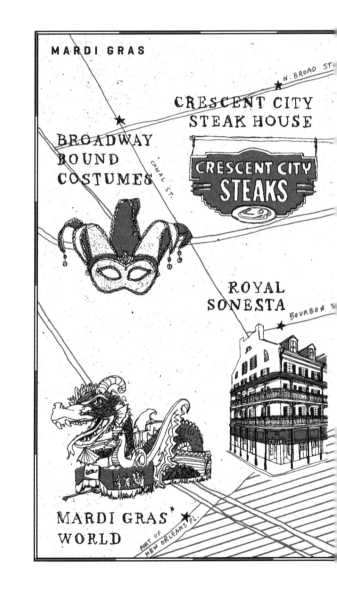

CRESCENT CITY
STEAK HOUSE

N. BROAD ST.

BROADWAY
BOUND
COSTUMES

CANAL ST.

ROYAL
SONESTA

BOURBON S

MARDI GRAS
WORLD

PORT OF
NEW ORLEANS PL.

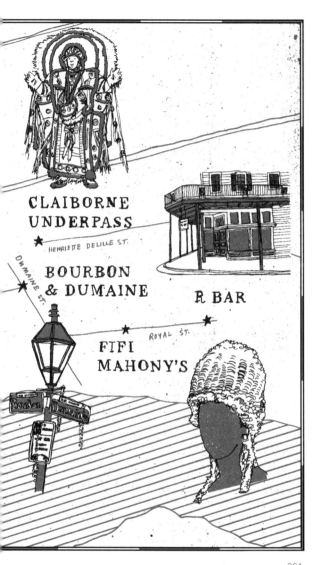

CLAIBORNE
UNDERPASS

★
HENRIETTE DELILLE ST.

BOURBON
& DUMAINE

R BAR

★
ROYAL ST.

FIFI
MAHONY'S

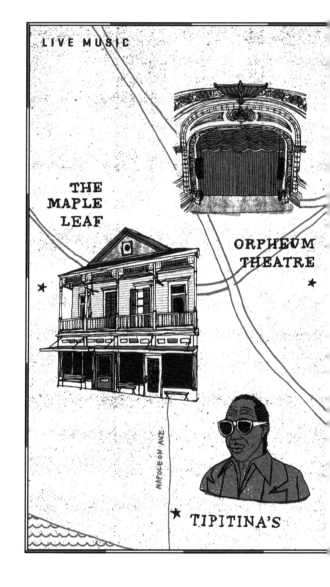

LIVE MUSIC

THE
MAPLE
LEAF

ORPHEUM
THEATRE

NAPOLEON AVE.

TIPITINA'S

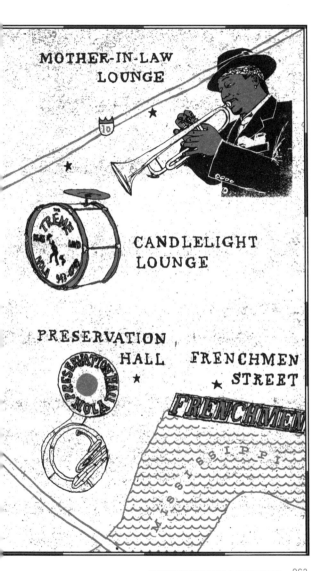

MOTHER-IN-LAW
LOUNGE

CANDLELIGHT
LOUNGE

PRESERVATION
HALL

FRENCHMEN
STREET

LIVE MUSIC

While other cities shout claim to America's live music capital, New Orleans shows there isn't even a contest.

TIPITINA'S

Professor Longhair's home venue until his death in 1980, then known as the 501 Club. Now one of the country's premier venues thanks to members of Galactic giving it new life. Often a site of surprise late-night sets during Jazz Fest. *501 Napoleon Ave*

CANDLELIGHT LOUNGE

The spot to catch the Treme Brass Band, one of the city's best with an impressive alumni list. Order the "set up," a half-pint of booze, a bowl of ice and some plastic cups. *925 N Robertson St*

MAPLE LEAF BAR

Far uptown, yes, but an evening here is worth the voyage. George Porter Jr. [The Meters] and Rebirth Brass Band both regular resident performers. Fans of the piano genius James Booker know this Oak Street bar as hallowed ground. *8316 Oak St*

PRESERVATION HALL

Still the best venue to see traditional jazz in New Orleans since honeymooners Allan and Sandra Jaffe founded it in 1961. Their son Ben leads the hall's namesake group on tuba. *726 St Peter*

ORPHEUM

A downtown beaux arts beauty restored after it was flooded during Hurricane Katrina. Double Dealer, a vaudeville-inspired bar, downstairs. *129 Roosevelt Way*

KERMIT'S TREMÉ MOTHER-IN-LAW LOUNGE

Once the cosmic headquarters of Ernie K-Doe, self-described "Emperor of the Universe." Now owned by trumpeter Kermit Ruffins, who also barbecues out back. *1500 N Claiborne Ave*

FRENCHMEN STREET

Some of the city's best clubs all on one stretch. Crawl from Snug Harbor to d.b.a. to the Spotted Cat. Street-corner bands too.

PLAY ON *A secluded grove of interactive, musical "treehouses" at the Ninth Ward's edge, Music Box Village is half venue, half playground for both world-renowned artists and preschoolers.*

PORCHES & COURTYARDS

From hotel piazzas to lush gardens and hidden oases, these are the spots to sit a spell.

JEWEL OF THE SOUTH

New Orleans cocktail maestro Chris Hannah has his own bar now, a cornflower-shuttered Creole cottage complete with a frond-shaded patio. Brandy crustas all around. *1026 St Louis St*

COLUMNS

The city's power porch. Cubs the Poet sometimes types spontaneous verse on his typewriter while movers and shakers sip jungle birds and snack on Coquette-made small plates under chartreuse umbrellas. *3811 St Charles Ave*

SAINT-GERMAIN

A French wine bar with a DIY spirit, its facade belies the verdant courtyard that becomes a twinkly paradise as the sun sets behind the loquat tree. One of the best lists in town with half-priced bottles on Wednesdays. *3054 St Claude Ave*

SECRET GARDENS OF THE VIEUX CARRÉ TOUR

Take a sanctioned, self-guided peek behind the timeworn walls and filigreed gates of the French Quarter. Small space inspo before it was cool. *patioplanters.net*

CAFE DEGAS

A casual-cool Bayou St. John bistro and neighborhood haunt. The "sidecar" two-top below the green neon sign on the side porch makes for a romantic respite. *3127 Esplanade Ave*

HOTEL SAINT VINCENT

Wraparound verandas on this once orphanage, now sprawling Italianate property encourage one to recline and gather their wits a while. *1507 Magazine St*

BEAUBOURG THEATRE

A downtown dream. Walk to the postage-stamp courtyard through the theater's cafe, Fourth Wall Coffee. *614 Gravier St*

LOCAL BEAUTY *For more stunning scenes, enchanting and eerie, wander from the Marigny Opera House—once a church, now a performance space—to St. Roch Cemetery and look for the ex-votos left in the chapel.*

HOTEL
SAINT ★
VINCENT

CAFE
DEGAS

ESPLANADE AVE.

SAINT
VINCENT
CLUB HOTEL POOL
RESTAURANT.

CAFÉ
Degas

10

THE
COLUMNS

ST. CHARLES AVE.

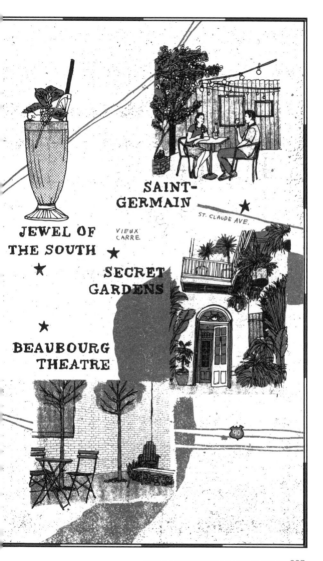

JEWEL OF
THE SOUTH
★

SAINT-
GERMAIN
★

ST. CLAUDE AVE.

VIEUX
CARRE

★
SECRET
GARDENS

★
BEAUBOURG
THEATRE

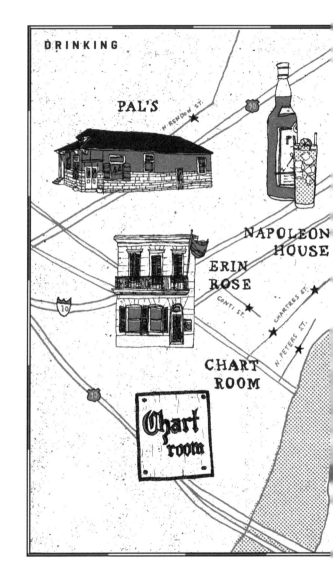

DRINKING

PAL'S

NAPOLEON
HOUSE

ERIN
ROSE

CHART
ROOM

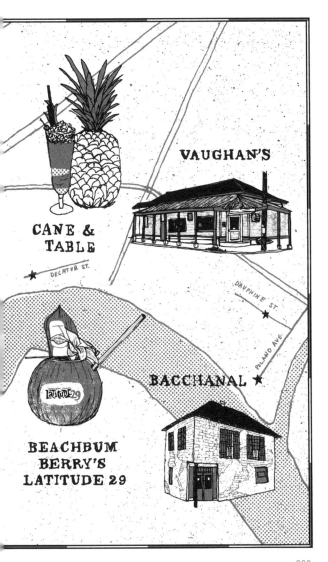

VAUGHAN'S

CANE &
TABLE

DECATUR ST.

DAUPHINE ST.

POLAND AVE.

BACCHANAL ★

BEACHBUM
BERRY'S
LATITUDE 29

DRINKING

Nowhere else are neighborhood dives just as important to local culture as luxurious, history-steeped cocktail bars.

ERIN ROSE

Inside at the bar with a frozen Irish coffee, Bourbon Street will seem a world away instead of mere steps. In the back, Killer PoBoys fixes new-wave variations like rum-glazed pork belly or sweet potato. *811 Conti St*

VAUGHAN'S LOUNGE

Possibly New Orleans' best neighborhood bar. A rusty shell of its past life as a grocery. Live music, crock-pot meals and mojitos under a rainbow sky of papel picado. *4229 Dauphine St*

CANE & TABLE

A heavenly, Hemingway-esque haunt. Expertly made tropical cocktails are the deal here, down to the frozen piña colada. So be extra and get it served in the coconut. *1113 Decatur St*

NAPOLEON HOUSE

How old is this place? Napoleon was supposed to spend the night here. Take refuge at the porticoed table with a chilly, cucumber-garnished Pimm's cup. *500 Chartres St*

PAL'S LOUNGE

Another neighborhood treasure, this one with regular pop-ups by new NOLA talent and a resident chicken named Cheeto. *949 N Rendon St*

BACCHANAL

Ball out on this bottle list, and watch the barges and container ships glide past the levee. The kitchen cranks killer tapas too. *600 Poland Ave*

BEACHBUM BERRY'S LATITUDE 29

Top-notch tiki drinks made by scholar of the genre and owner Jeff "Beachbum" Berry. *321 N Peters St*

THE CHART ROOM

A cash-only corner dive that's seen it all. Use your change to feed the jukebox. *300 Chartres St*

SIP THE STANDARD *Many of the country's classic cocktails were invented in New Orleans, including the Sazerac, hurricane, brandy crusta, Ramos gin fizz, Vieux Carré and absinthe frappé.*

HISTORIC HOMES

With three centuries' worth of architecture, New Orleans is a treasure trove of houses and the stories they contain.

DOULLUT STEAMBOAT HOUSES

Two remarkable examples of steamboat architecture, echoing the ornate vessels on the Mississippi River. The first one was built by Mary Doullut, the first woman with a river pilot license in Louisiana. Survived Katrina. *400 and 503 Egania*

MILTENBERGER HOUSES

A French Quarter icon. Necklaced in ferns, this Royal Street building with wrought-iron balconies is actually three row houses built by Marie Aimee Miltenberger for each of her sons. *900-910 Royal St*

KID ORY'S HOUSE

Edward "Kid" Ory moved to the city on his 21st birthday and went on to play with Louis Armstrong, and his namesake band revived interest in New Orleans jazz during the '40s. The Preservation Resource Center restored his red cottage. *2135 Jackson Ave*

SMITH WENDELL GREEN HOME

Saved but still sitting on cinder blocks, this mansion belonged to S.W. Green, a powerful Black businessman who constructed the Pythian Temple downtown in 1909, which has recently been revived. *Banks St and S Rocheblave St*

MILTON H. LATTER LIBRARY

This palatial public library was once home to a silent movie star, horse-racetrack owner and, early on, some livestock. *5120 St Charles Ave*

DEGAS HOUSE

Edgar Degas stayed here only a year, but it's said to be where he dreamt up a revolutionary style. A rare French government landmark on U.S. soil. *2306 Esplanade Ave*

THE GARDEN DISTRICT

Thirteen blocks long, packed with the city's grandest homes. Claims once and present residents John Goodman, Anne Rice, Julia Reed. *St Charles Ave to Magazine St*

LOCAL EXPERT *Geographer and Tulane University professor Richard Campanella has written 12 books on New Orleans, from a history of Bourbon Street to a deep dive into the city's urban planning.*

SMITH WENDELL
GREEN MANSION ★

KID ORY'S
HOUSE
★

MILTON H.
LATTER
LIBRARY
★

ST. CHARLES AVE.

★

THE GARDEN
DISTRICT

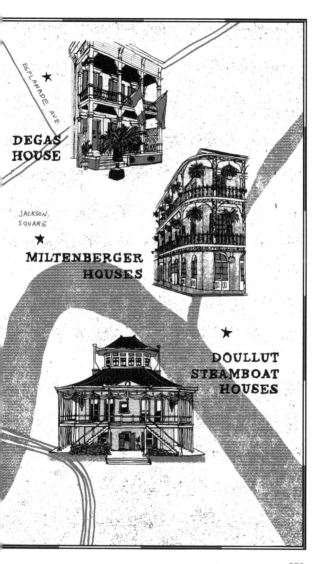

ESPLANADE AVE.

★

**DEGAS
HOUSE**

JACKSON.
SQUARE
★

**MILTENBERGER
HOUSES**

★

**DOULLUT
STEAMBOAT
HOUSES**

INTERVIEWS

---

*Thirteen conversations with locals of note about
oyster shucking, music, historic preservation, writing,
shrimp, saxophone repair, second lines and more*

THOMAS STEWART

OTSTER SHUCKER

I'VE BEEN AT Pascal's Manale for 28 years—25 of them shucking oysters.

FIVE DAYS a week. Three in the afternoon until we close.

I'M AN ARIES. The day before I came in for the job, I checked my horoscope and it said, "You're coming to a job you're going to be at for a long time."

I STARTED OUT washing dishes.

THE CHEF ASKED me if I knew how to handle the knife. My mama taught me to never say you can't do something till you try. So I said, I'm gonna try.

I'M NOT A big fan of oysters. Never was. I don't dislike the taste, but it's just a texture thing.

I'D RATHER OPEN them and see other people enjoy them.

SEE THIS OYSTER? It's dead, lost all its energy.

I TAP ON them to see if they sound hollow. Then I feel for the opening at the front.

I USE THE Dexter-Russell with the plastic handle. I live by 'em.

THIS KNIFE FITS my hand perfectly.

SOMETIMES THEY snap in the heat of the moment, like the cereal, snap, crackle, pop. I got two backups in case.

I FILE THEM about twice a week, very gently.

YOU DON'T WANT the knife to turn into an ice pick. I just want an edge so when I hit the muscle I get a clean cut.

I STILL WORK in the kitchen when they need me, but my main drag is shucking in the front.

WHEN IT GETS hot, I rub ice on my wrists to keep cool.

THAT TATTOO right there, that's my brand. Uptown T with two crossed oyster knives.

WALTER ISAACSON

BIOGRAPHER, WRITER

I WAS RAISED in the same house on Napoleon Avenue where my great-granduncle lived.

VERY EARLY ON I had a sense that New Orleans was a special place.

WHEN WE STOOD on the levee of the Mississippi or walked in the French Quarter or fished down the pipeline canals, I knew that it was the most wonderful place on earth.

MY FAMILY'S BEEN in New Orleans for many generations. They were mainly engineers or doctors.

WE HAD THE FIRST residential swimming pool in New Orleans, because my dad and granduncle built it as a way to test cooling coils for air-conditioning systems.

MY BEST FRIEND'S uncle was Walker Percy.

HE LIVED IN Covington on the Bogue Falaya, where we used to water ski in the summer.

I REMEMBER ASKING his daughter Ann one day, when we were about 10 years old, "What does your dad do?" And she said, "Well, he's a writer." I didn't know you could be a writer as a job.

THESE ARE THE best six words: "Let me tell you a story."

ONE TIME, DR. PERCY told me, "There are two types of people that come out of Louisiana: Preachers and storytellers. For heaven's sake, be a storyteller. The world has too many preachers."

I'VE BEEN ABLE to meet a lot of smart people in my life, both in college and as a reporter. And at some point I came to realize that smart people are a dime a dozen.

WHAT MAKES SOMEONE a genius is the ability to think differently. In my writing I often explore the roots of creativity. And whether it's da Vinci or Steve Jobs or Benjamin Franklin, their genius comes from a playful curiosity, and it led them to find patterns in the world.

IN THE HISTORY of New Orleans, the genius who comes to my mind is Louis Armstrong.

HE EMBODIED the diversity of New Orleans, steeped in broad traditions. The Sanctified Church, blues from the plantations, the French Opera House and Creole foxtrot orchestras, the drumming in Congo Square. All those sources flowed together to form Louis Armstrong.

THE CITY THAT reminds me the most of New Orleans is Venice, Italy. Each with its beauties and its challenges.

BOTH OF THEM are cities of masks, where people like to fantasize and pretend. Both of them are cities of great creativity and eerie beauty. People give in and get to pretend to be who they want to be.

LOUIS ARMSTRONG often wore the smile on his face as a mask. It allowed him to present a joyful exterior to the world, but to keep a little something mysterious inside.

A FEW YEARS AGO, Mitch Landrieu asked Wynton Marsalis and myself to be co-chairs of the tricentennial celebration for the city.

WYNTON CALLED ME up and said that he'd do it if I would do it, but on one condition.

HE SAID, "I want you to help me convince people to take down the statue of Robert E. Lee." And I said, "I've driven around that circle thousands of times and I've never paid much attention to who was standing on the top of that tall column." And Wynton says, "I do. I pay attention to it."

THERE'S STILL A void at the top of the column. People keep saying, What should we put there?

I THINK WE should leave it like it is, empty, a void.

IT'S A REMINDER that our city was able to have a difficult discussion and come out the other side. How powerful is that?

I'VE OFTEN THOUGHT of writing a biography of Louis Armstrong as a way to convey the complexities of our city. But I'm not sure I fully understand what's behind Louis Armstrong's mask of a smile.

I HOPE SOMEDAY to write the book with Wynton Marsalis. I could gather all the information about Armstrong's story; Wynton could explain what it means.

SANDY NGUYEN

COMMUNITY ADVOCATE

MY FAMILY came over from Vietnam in 1979.

THE DAY WE came, Dad got on a boat and became somebody's deckhand.

MY MOM STARTED shucking oysters within a week, and worked two, sometimes three shifts a day. My eldest brother, who was 10, took care of us.

I STARTED translating at 14. I did everything from court translation to immigration.

THE THREE main businesses in the Asian community are nails and fishing and grocery stores.

AFTER KATRINA, we formed Coastal Communities Consulting.

YOU KNOW THERE'S great seafood, but you don't know the people or the tough work behind the seafood.

WE HAVE OVER 1,200 clients, all commercial fishermen and surrounding businesses, like a gas station or the little bait shop.

THE VIETNAMESE, the Cambodians, the Americans—it's all the same. They all need the same type of grant assistance, loan help and business management.

ASIANS BUST THEIR tails to do this so that their kids can go to school and have a nice corporate job. The Americans, they hand down the fishing by generation.

AFTER THE BP SPILL, we saved people about $2.5 million in legal fees that they put back into their boats.

IT'S THE uncertainty, the not knowing. A lot of people got sick. You could see the stress in the fishermen.

I'M NOT A scientist or biologist, but I know the shrimp is not there like it used to be.

WHEN MY DAD retired, he sold his shrimp boat to my husband. So I'm a fisherman's wife too.

LYNN RIVERS

TEACHER

JUST 'CAUSE it works in New York doesn't mean it will work in New Orleans.

LOUISIANA HAS BEEN struggling a long time with education, period.

HERE'S HOW I see it: Schools don't make people. People make schools.

I WENT TO John F. Kennedy High. It's no longer in existence.

MR. PARKER. He was a really good listener. That, to me, makes all the difference.

THE SYSTEM was more orderly back then. Things feel all spread out today.

I HAVE TWO daughters. Nine and 17. They go to KIPP Central City Academy and Warren Easton Senior High.

BY THE GRACE of God, we got in on the first try.

OUR DAYS START at 5:30 a.m.

OUTSIDE OF SCHOOL, my youngest attends NOLA Ballet, karate, the majorettes. My oldest is at the Trombone Shorty Academy at Tulane too. How do they do it? Mama. That's how.

AN IDLE MIND is the devil's workshop. That's what the old folks used to say.

NO IPHONES at the dinner table.

YOU CAN'T prevent everything. But you better believe I'm going to try.

TAKE AN INTEREST in New Orleans culture. Because if you don't understand us, how can you teach our children?

SOME OF THE Teach For America teachers are great. Some, I wonder about the motives. Is teaching a calling, or are they thinking of paying off college loans?

THE GREAT Experiment. That sums up New Orleans education right there.

DON RICHMOND

NEIGHBORHOOD HISTORIAN

MY NAME IS Don Richmond, and what else is it what you want? I don't hear well.

MY GREAT-GRANDPARENTS came to New Orleans on their honeymoon.

I CAME HERE because I read a book, *Fabulous New Orleans*, by Lyle Saxon.

THAT WAS IN the '60s. I lived in the French Quarter, in a building on Decatur Street.

IN THOSE DAYS, the Mafia were very much in evidence. They had bookie joints, they had prostitution, they had bars. You name it, they were in it.

EVENTUALLY, you pay a price for everything.

I BOUGHT THIS house [in Faubourg Marigny] in 1977. It was a ruin.

IT WAS BUILT, probably around 1825, by a woman whose name was Rosette Rochon, a free woman of color.

SHE WAS BORN a slave in Mobile, Alabama—her father was the first white shipbuilder there. Before he died, he freed Rosette's mother, a mulatto slave, and the children he'd had with her, and he gave all the children a heifer.

WHAT DO YOU DO with a heifer? You breed them. And Rosette became a businesswoman.

SHE OWNED a chain of grocery stores. She built houses. She was a licensed butcher. She loaned money, at interest.

IN 1863, she died after almost 100 years. New Orleans was bad, it was the Civil War.

THEY POURED the molasses in the streets to keep the Yankees from getting it.

IT WAS A man's world. For a woman, a so-called single woman, to succeed was a miracle. Rosette was exceptional.

GEORGE PORTER JR.

MUSICIAN

AS A KID I heard brass bands a lot because there was a social aid and pleasure club called the Jolly Bunch down the street from our home.

ONCE EVERY MONTH, if not twice, there would be a funeral, so we got to see street bands march by.

I WAS AN altar boy in school. I knew the whole mass in Latin.

MY GRANDMOTHER GAVE me an acoustic guitar on my eighth birthday, but my mother said the rule was I had to take lessons.

I DIDN'T HAVE any problem with that. My problem was my teacher. He was teaching me cowboy songs, you know, like "Red River Valley" and "Home, Home on the Range."

THE METERS PLAYED together for three years before we got into Sea-Saint Studio with Allen Toussaint. We had already developed a statement sound. I think that's why he was drawn to us.

THE ARTISTS WERE almost never in the studio with us. I think Patti LaBelle came in after we tracked the "Lady Marmalade" record. But Robert Palmer was there. And Dr. John. We were in the studio with him for two records.

OPENING FOR THE Rolling Stones in Paris in 1976, the first 10 minutes was very uncomfortable. It could have been dangerous because people started to throw things.

MICK JAGGER WENT out on stage and, I'm assuming, told them in their language to shut the fuck up. Listen to these guys.

THEY STAYED ON stage with us as we sang "Fire on the Bayou." The audience quieted down and gave us a wonderful applause.

WHEN WE PLAYED the first Jazz Fest after Hurricane Katrina, the fact that it was even pulled off was really a surprise. It took local people who were living in trailers and stuff to make it

happen. I wasn't even back in my home then.

....

I THINK MY newest album with the Runnin' Pardners is probably the best recording I've done to date.

....

AS A YOUNG guy then, and even now, I still get into a van and drive to go on tour. At the end of a tour this past weekend, there weren't affordable hotel rooms in Key West, so we got some coffee and drove 16 hours home.

....

I WOULD NEVER ask my guys to do anything I wouldn't do. Maybe next year, I might have a different attitude. But today, I'm 73 and I'm still working with my guys.

MIKE LORINO

RIVER PILOT

THIRTY TO 35 ships a day. Some four football fields long and 45 feet deep.

....

WE PILOT THE ships from the Gulf of Mexico to Pilottown.

....

I MET MY late wife when we were 14 and 15. Her name was Donna, and her father was a river pilot.

....

WE WERE married and I went down the river.

....

IT WAS MOSTLY sons that were getting in, and I was a "son-in-law" so I was considered an outsider.

....

RIGHT NOW there's 47 of us.

....

THE ONLY WAY to get to our stations is by boat. It's marsh. No city, no nothing.

....

NARROW AND shallow. Both those things are hard for ships.

....

AND IN APRIL, the current goes to eight knots. All that snow up north comes right out the mouth.

WHEN I STARTED, you relied on the radio. And you looked out the window at the lights and knew where you were.

....

A LOT OF THE trees are gone. It's open water. Cypress, oak. They're getting all washed away.

....

LOUISIANA LOSES a football field of land every two hours.

....

THE ENVIRONMENTALISTS say that in 50 years, the Gulf will be up to New Orleans.

....

DURING WORLD WAR II, two ships were torpedoed by subs just off Burrwood. The pilots could hear them come up and take on air. That's how close the Germans were to us.

....

THE BEST THING? Get on the lee side of the storm and ride it out.

....

YOU NEED A college education and pretty good nerves.

....

DO I FISH? No. I've had enough of the water.

ANGIE SHELTON

HOTEL HOUSEKEEPER

I WAS BORN in New Orleans.

MY MOTHER DIED when I was nine, so all seven of us went to go live with my grandparents on Burgundy between Toulouse and St. Peters.

MY GRANDMOTHER cleaned houses and had a restaurant on Bourbon.

AS KIDS, we had to work. We sold cans, newspapers, rags, bottle glass. Every morning at five o'clock, we'd go through the trash.

MY DAUGHTERS have it so easy.

MY HUSBAND has been on Bourbon Street for 37 years as a musician. He plays the bass guitar in the house band for Fat Catz.

I BEEN housekeeping manager at the hotel for 29 years. Two of my brothers work here too. Aaron and Farrell, the bellman and the maintenance guy.

WE DEAL WITH a lot of hair. There's hair on the bed or hair in the tub—that's the most frequent complaint.

HOW DO YOU know it didn't fall out your head?

THE HOTEL BUILDING used to be a morgue, and some guests claim to have seen ghosts.

A MAN KILLED himself in 226. Put blue tarp paper on the windowsill so we couldn't see in and shot himself in the bathtub.

I DO BELIEVE in ghosts, but I never seen anything here.

WE SEND OUT the comforters to be dry cleaned every six months. Should be every three.

IT DON'T TAKE a rocket scientist to clean. You just gotta be a clean person yourself.

ONE TIME a guy had a bowel movement, but he didn't flush. He complained, and I said, "I thought you wanted to keep it, so we left it for you." Nobody's here to flush your shit.

CALVIN DUNCAN

LAWYER, ADVOCATE

MY MOM DIED when I was seven, so we bounced around a lot.

WHEN I WAS 14, I wanted to look nice in school, so I started shoplifting. That decision ruined my life.

I GOT CAUGHT and they took my mugshot.

A GIRL and a boy were at a bus stop on Esplanade and Roman. Two guys tried to rob them and winded up killing the boyfriend.

THEY PUT IT on Crimestoppers, and someone called in and said the person who did the crime was "a Negro male named Calvin Duncan."

MY AUNTIE called me and said I was on the news. I said that couldn't be. She kept telling me I was, I was, I was.

I WAS 19 years old. And I had just started the process of joining the military. That was my dream.

THE STATE sought the death penalty. My trial lasted one day.

PROSECUTERS AND POLICE have the authority. They decide.

I DIDN'T KNOW what was going on. I wasn't educated.

MY FAMILY TESTIFIED to where I was on that night. I was at home painting the house for a birthday party the next day.

THE DETECTIVE in the case intentionally lied, and we eventually got the evidence to prove it.

YOU HAVE hope, you believe that things will work out. That they'll call your name and say, "We made a mistake."

EVEN AFTER you're found guilty, you believe the system will work itself out.

MY PROSECUTOR didn't agree with the Supreme Court that said he had to share exculpatory evidence.

I SPENT 24 years at Angola.

Twenty-three years I was an inmate lawyer.

....

WHAT GAVE THEM the authority to do what they did to me? The law.

....

THE POLICE department wanted $25 to send me a report. But you only making four cents an hour in prison.

....

WHAT'S THE ODDS of you getting those documents?

....

SISYPHUS WAS condemned by Zeus to roll a boulder up a steep hill, forever.

....

THEY SAY OUR court doors are open. That's bullshit. To get through all of them, you have to be Superman.

....

WHEN KATRINA hit, we weren't worried about the city. I was worried about my documents getting destroyed.

....

THIS ONE DA, his name is Jim Williams. He sent six people to Death Row and he had these trophies with their photographs on them.

....

TODAY, FIVE OF those six people are now free.

....

THERE'S A GUY, Reginald Adams, accused of killing a police officer's wife. And the same police officer remarried and had killed his second wife. Everybody knew. But Reginald was in prison for 34 years for it.

....

HE WAS released in May.

....

WHEN THE assistant prosecutor who prosecuted me became the judge over my case, the God of Hope left me.

....

HE SAID THAT I should have found the evidence 30 years ago.

....

GOD STEPS IN when the impossible needs to be done. Why he didn't do anything sooner, I don't know.

....

IN THE END, I still had to plead guilty to get out.

....

THAT'S THE system. I could continue to tell the truth and I might stay in prison, or say the magic words and I'd be out.

....

THEY GIVE you a $10 check when they let you out. I never cashed it.

....

ME AND MY daughter are close. And my grandson. His name is Josiah.

....

Duncan began law school in
Portland, Oregon, in 2020.

MARTIN KRUSCHE

SAXOPHONE REPAIRMAN

I'VE ALWAYS been repairing instruments. I started with my own horn. I took my first sax apart before I could even play.

I WAS BORN in Munich and studied at a conservatory in Germany, but I moved here in 1995.

ONLY SAXOPHONES. I don't do clarinets or trumpets or flutes.

HERE IN New Orleans I am the guy everybody goes to.

BECAUSE I PLAY, I know the potential of an instrument and whether it's working as well as it can.

I MAKE MY living from two-thirds repair, one-third gigging.

SAXES MOLD to match their player.

THE VIBRATIONS have an effect on the inner structure. Over time, it shakes off the lacquer, becomes more and more resonant.

A PLAYED instrument is responsive and malleable.

JANUARY THROUGH April is my peak time. This is when Mardi Gras happens, Jazz Fest. Everyone's making money and getting their horn fixed.

A SAXOPHONE IS a woodwind, not a brass.

PEOPLE SEND horns from all over the country.

I LIKE Snug Harbor on Frenchmen. They cultivate a quiet room.

I REPAIR dents, broken springs, rusty parts, but 90 percent of what I do is pad replacement.

SOMEONE ALWAYS has an emergency. They just flew into town, dropped their horn on the flight, playing a gig that night.

A COMPLETE OVERHAUL costs $650. It takes a week.

YOU HAVE TO keep the player in mind. We do this now, we do the rest later.

GABRIELLE BEGUE

ARCHITECTURAL HISTORIAN

THE FIELD OF preservation combines everything I love.

DAD'S FAMILY came over from southwest France in the 1870s. My great-great grandfather, Jean Begue, was escaping the Franco-Prussian War.

HE BECAME a butcher. His brother Hippolyte, a bartender.

THE GALATOIRE'S family is from the same part of France.

JEAN WON the lottery, $10,000 in Cuban gold, and his wife forced him to invest in real estate. He bought 16 buildings and built a few more.

THAT'S BEEN A part of my life forever, taking care of [my family's] buildings, all in the French Quarter and the Marigny.

OUR ARCHITECTURE comes from France, from Spain, from the Caribbean. How they're combined is what's unique.

OUR FAMILY owned a restaurant near the French Market called Madame Begue's. It claims to have invented brunch.

FOURTEEN COURSES. Drinking with every single one.

IT NEVER GOT fancy. It just became famous.

WE'RE A Galatoire's family. My parents were the people who came for lunch and stayed through dinner. Cesar was our waiter.

BEFORE MY parents bought it in 1978, our house was a brothel.

IT WAS CALLED House of the Rising Sun, not from *Easy Rider.*

WHEN MY MOM was very pregnant with me, she would still get guys ringing the door.

WE STAYED through Katrina.

I SAW ENTIRE tree branches just flying by, zipping past Elysian Fields into the Marigny. The sound of the wind was like a freight train.

SUSAN SPICER

CHEF

IF SOMEONE ever asks me what to order at Bayona, I'll always say sweetbreads. Just to test them.

CONFIDENCE is important.

WHEN I STARTED, I was five years older than half the cooks in my kitchen.

I DIDN'T HAVE an old Cajun grandmother. My mom was from Copenhagen.

THE BEST CHEFS dig the work.

I'M ONE OF seven kids, and my dad was in the Navy.

A&G CAFETERIA. That was about it for eating out.

MOM HAD THIS set of mahogany bowls she would put the condiments in. Chopped eggs, scallions, peanuts, fried onions, chutney, all for her beef and curry.

I SHOWED A Culinary Institute brochure to my dad and he laughed. I was just aimless and looking for something.

I ALWAYS loved music—and musicians—but I had no talent.

TO GROW, to get better, you have to do what you think you can't do.

LIKE COMING back and putting on a comfortable pair of old shoes. The Big Easy, it feels good, comfortable.

WHEN I STARTED working for a chef, there was an epiphany.

I JUST SAID, finally, finally. This is satisfying everything.

I HAVE THIS *New Yorker* cartoon on my door. It's a woman chef standing at the table of a big-chested business man. "Oh, you're the chef? Well, my compliments anyway."

A FRENCH CHEF came in and said, "Your cooking reminds me of my grandmother." To me, that was awesome.

AT THE END of the night, just give me my glass of wine.

VICTOR HARRIS

MARDI GRAS INDIAN CHIEF

I'VE WORN A Mardi Gras Indian suit for 50 years.

WHAT'S THE best one? The next one! You try to top that suit every year.

I WAS BORN into it. Being a kid, it was more exciting than Christmas.

THE CHIEF HAS to approve of you being in the tribe. Growing up, I had the legendary chief, the late great Tootie Montana, just a couple of yards from me.

I WAS RAISED on Villere and Pauger Street.

FOR TWO, maybe three years, I sat around and watched them. I did little tedious things, but I never picked up the needle.

ONE DAY THEY told me, Come on, let's try and do this. I said, "Man no, I don't think I can do that." He said, "Oh, you been watching me long enough, it's time for you to start sewing." So that's how it all began.

THEN FOUR YEARS after, he said, "Why don't you make you a suit?"

MYSELF, I ALWAYS been a colorful person. Even in school I was always good at mixing and matching colors.

THAT WAS MY first suit, white with American eagles on it. Feathers, plumes, tips or fluff they call them, regular things, beads, pearls.

IN ORDER TO create my designs, I have to go to the spirits, to the elders, to the ancestors.

I THINK OF the African culture more than the Native Indian culture now.

ST. JOSEPH'S NIGHT and Mardi Gras Day are the two times we put our suits on.

NOWADAYS, they just jump up and down and say, "I'm a chief." But they never worn a suit before. Those guys aren't respected. They haven't earned it.

I AM THE spirit of Fi Yi Yi. I truly believe in it. I don't mess with the spirits.

....

TRADITIONALLY we had to burn the suits, to give them back to the spirits. But I started saving them in the mid-'80s.

....

I'VE GOT 15 or 20 at the Backstreet Cultural Museum.

THIS WAS segregation, so Black people had their own Mardi Gras in their own community, and a lot of this was unheard of by tourists.

....

SPY BOY IS the person who's maybe two blocks ahead of the tribe, like a scout. He's looking for other tribes. Then you have the flag boy. He's a block behind the spy boy and a block ahead of the tribe. Then you have the wild man, he's just ripping and running, back and forth, making a lot of noise, whooping and hollering. They always find the craziest guy to be the wild man.

....

IN MY DAYS, when I saw the wild man coming, I used to run.

....

WHEN WE SEE another tribe, the drums go to beating. We're about to go into battle.

THE CHIEF is the chief. The chief is always the chief.

....

I DONE BEEN in a bunch of scuffles, but it's like a football game as far as I'm concerned.

....

CLAIBORNE AVENUE is the neutral ground. You used to have them big ole pretty oak trees until they came through with the I-10 and destroyed the land.

....

IT TOOK AWAY the Mardi Gras because that was Carnival for the Black people.

....

PEOPLE JUST would go there and sit under those big ole beautiful trees. It was like every family had a tree, for picnics, for Sunday afternoon, for relaxation, whatever. That's how beautiful it was. And every family named a tree.

....

THAT WAS the place, that was the sacred ground. I'm telling you, everyone had a tree.

....

ONE OF MY major buddies recently passed away. He sat at the table with me for 47 years. I don't even know if I want to make it without him. We had a hell of a journey together.

STORIES

*Essays and selected writing from
noted New Orleans voices*

THE VANISHING BLACK BARS OF NEW ORLEANS

Written by **L. KASIMU HARRIS** | **ON MOTHER'S DAY WEEKEND** of 2021, my wife and I staycationed at The Roosevelt Hotel, a historic property from 1893 in downtown New Orleans, famous for the Sazerac bar in the lobby and its ties to Louisiana Governor Huey P. Long, also known as "The Kingfish." We had a wonderful escape save for two things. At check-in we were given a list of restaurants: some revered classics, others the expected, overrated tourist traps, but none Black-owned. Missing from that list were renowned institutions like Dooky Chase's Restaurant [1941] where the late chef Leah Chase fed U.S. Presidents; Willie Mae's Scotch House [1957], and its two locations to savor America's best fried chicken; and Compère Lapin [2015], where chef/co-owner Nina Compton received the James Beard Award for Best Chef: South in 2018. And in our room, and those of everyone else staying there, the hotel's infomercial channel advised guests of a plethora of things to do during their stay in New Orleans—but again, it never mentioned Black-owned businesses or directed visitors to the centers of Black culture.

In my mind, a familiar refrain rang out: Fuck New Orleans. She is a temptress. A femme fatale who's run the same game for 300 years. Yet, we, I, still fall for her. Don't save her, she don't want to be saved. Don't get me wrong, I fucking love New Orleans. But Black folks' unrequited love with this city is generational and unrelenting. And I still find new ways to be disappointed and disrespected while I am seduced and attached.

New Orleans markets its distinct culture around the world, but there is a modicum, at best, of encouragement for visitors to experience the inextricable root of it, Black culture, once they arrive. The powers that be within the tourism industry have long peddled the imagery of Black Masking Indians, also known as Mardi Gras Indians, and the city's many social aid and pleasure clubs, with their famous second lines. But still today they remain reluctant to promote the places those traditions emanate from: New Orleans' Black neighborhoods and, specifically, their bars and lounges. In turn, these places miss out on the $9 billion that millions of visitors spend in the city on average every year.

Black spaces in New Orleans are as old as the city itself, and many of today's standing bars reach back to the civil rights movement. Although demolished in 1965, Economy Hall was completed all the way back in 1836, and served as what was said to be a Carnegie Hall-like space for Black and Creole people, with debates, dances and performances—including some by Kid Ory—among other functions. Both those from the past and those standing today are a respite from the racial and economic inequities outside of the Black community, a place where one could get a drink with dignity or slow-drag on the dance floor or just talk.

I still had the sting of that staycation in me when I walked inside Sportsman's Corner on a Monday afternoon. Mark Reynolds, 49, sat at the bar sipping on a Modelo. A couple perched a few stools down, playing video poker and sipping on frozen daiquiris. The 6 p.m. local news, WWL channel 4, was muted on a large flat-screen TV that illuminated a cadre of old men who huddled around a table, drinking beer and kibitzing. Music blared from a jukebox. The news turned to *Jeopardy*.

"This barroom, especially for a lot of old guys, it feeds the soul," Reynolds said. "Outside of family and work, this is their safe haven. A lot of old guys live for this."

Reynolds has been a patron for about nine years. He's a member of Young Men Olympian Junior Benevolent Association, a 137-year-old organization that has had a longtime connection to Sportsman's Corner.

He said the bar's third-generation owner, Steven Elloie, has good prices, and sometimes for regulars, he'll buy them a drink. "But, I'll buy him a drink too," he said. "I don't care if he's the owner, that's my way of supporting Black businesses."

Since the late 1960s, New Orleans has experienced a bevy of hurricanes and recessions alongside rapid gentrification. Sportsman's Corner, at the intersection of Second and Dryades streets in Central City, has endured it all. Although just a couple blocks away from the picturesque turn-of-the-century mansions on oak-lined St. Charles Avenue, Central City has traditionally consisted of modest homes long lived in by working-class Black people. This bar is the epicenter of Uptown New Orleans' Black cultural traditions, and its walls are decorated with photographs of various social aid and pleasure clubs and Black Masking Indians.

When I spoke to Theresa Elloie in 2020, she said she knew that her late father, Louis Elloie, had initially rented the bar and believed he had purchased it as-is for $10,000 after it was damaged in a fire. Louis opened Sportsman's in the 1960s and ran it until his death in 2008 at 77 years old, and her first memories here start around when she was 13 or 14, when she could visit but wasn't allowed to sit at the bar. She said, nowadays, one sees more white people strolling with their dogs than Black people walking by and talked about all of the Black bars that have closed nearby. She mentioned a house across the street from Sportsman's had sold for $500,000, and an empty lot nearby went for $250,000.

"That money is of no value to me. They can't get this—ain't enough money!" Theresa said. "I used to get stuff in the mail [about selling]. Save your stamp, baby." Even as Black-owned bars around them and across town shutter, Theresa told me that Sportsman's Corner was here to stay.

"I've never considered selling. I want the doors to be forever open because [my father] sacrificed a lot. He put his health at risk and provided for his children," she said, referencing the fact that smoking in New Orleans bars and restaurants was only banned in 2015.

Steven, 41, worked alongside his grandfather for years, and since Hurricane Katrina has handled the bar's daily operations. While the front doors, wood paneling and bar remain original, Steven is perpetually responding to the contemporary desires of his patrons, evidenced by the recent addition of frozen daiquiris. Steven said he even planned to hire a white bartender. Sportsman's Corner remains an aberration for Black-owned bars by having three generations involved. And, if it's up to this family, it will continue.

"My two grandsons are already talking about who is next to run the bar," said Theresa.

More recently, Steven has wondered if the bar will survive the global pandemic. During another visit in late 2020, I sat on a red vinyl chair surrounded by some original furnishings installed when his grandfather established the bar. I asked questions with tears in my eyes and Steven answered with tears in his. Months earlier, in February when I sat in the same chair to talk to Theresa, it was just before Mardi Gras, when we reveled in the streets—unaware that we'd soon quarantine in

our homes. Theresa was working as an Uber driver, as Louis Ellioe had instilled the importance of multiple income streams with his children and grandchildren. She had complained about chest pain to Steven. Soon after, he brought her to the hospital, but he never saw or talked to her again. Two weeks later, in March 2020, she died from COVID-19.

"The way she passed, it was a hurting feeling" Steven said of his mother, who was just 63. "It just kind of killed my spirit."

On the door of the bar, stapled around a sun-faded Saints pennant, are obituaries from patrons who have also transitioned. When Louis died, a huge second line poured into his establishment, where mourners placed the casket on the bar and continued to celebrate his life. When Theresa died, because of the pandemic, it was a private service.

Today across the city, the Black bars that have endured through these unfathomable odds, like The Other Place, Bullet's Sports Bar, Hank's Bar, and Kermit's Tremé Mother-in-Law Lounge, have begun to sling drinks again and, in turn, preserve the culture. Bertha's Place Bar and Restaurant, Seal's Class Act and First & Last Stop Bar notably carry on the custom of Black bars owned by women.

Traditionally, on the Sundays approaching Mardi Gras Day, Tyrone Stevenson, Big Chief Pie of the Monogram Hunters, and his adult son Jeremy, lead Indian practice inside the First & Last Stop Bar at the intersection of Pauger and Marais streets in the South Seventh Ward. Tyrone, 50, has gone to Indian practices there since he was 12. Backed by the driving sound of mallets popping the drumheads on the two and four and the shaking of tambourine zills, Stevenson and the other chiefs sing a phrase between chants:

Shallow Water, Oh mama
Mardi Gras morning I won't kneel, I won't bow.
Shallow Water, Oh mama
'Cause I'm the big chief and I don't fall down
Shallow Water, Oh mama
Hooray, what they say
Shallow Water, Oh mama
Hooray, what they say
Shallow Water, Oh mama

Every year, that chant takes on more weight, never more so than this coming February 2022 when the city will celebrate Mardi Gras with an unprecedentedly pent-up spirit. In 2021, the mayor of New Orleans and a number of Big Chiefs from various Black Masking Indian tribes pleaded with other Indians to not mask on Carnival Day. Even so, some still did to quell their pain and escape seemingly endless isolation.

But as restrictions lift and visitors converge on the Big Easy streets, festivals return, conventions resume, and Mardi Gras krewes take to their routes, the tourists will more than likely flow back toward the places on the concierge's list, from the channel playing in the background of their hotel rooms. The Black culture bearers will persist, toil, and preserve their traditions—despite never recouping a return on their work. Will New Orleans ever realize the importance of these spaces? Will these Black bars continue to vanish or perserve? Save them, they want to be saved.

L. KASIMU HARRIS is a New Orleans-based artist who strives to tell stories of underrepresented communities in New Orleans and beyond. In 2020, Harris showed his photography at the Ford Foundation Gallery, Ogden Museum of Southern Art, August Wilson African American Cultural Center, and Crystal Bridges Museum of American Art. Also in 2020, his images and essay, "A Shot before Last Call: Capturing New Orleans' Vanishing Black Bars" were published in *The New York Times*. He has received artist residencies from the Center for Photography at Woodstock and the Joan Mitchell Center.

THE DEAD MUSEUM

Written by **RIEN FERTEL** | **IN NEW ORLEANS,** there is often more life in death than life in the living. T-shirts feature the lives of the recently deceased, while the newspapers' obituary pages rank second only to sports in popularity. Funeral homes charge extra to construct dramatic, lifelike funeral poses: standing on two feet, for example, or seated in a garden with a cigarette and glass of champagne in hand. Neighborhood streets often fill with jazz funerals that dance the departed souls into the afterlife. Weather, termites, poverty, even plain old indifference all cause our houses and hospitals and schools and levees to succumb to a state of atrophy that some find frustrating, but most often describe as picturesque and charming. Famously, the city is gradually sinking, an inch annually in some neighborhoods, while the coastline gets nearer by the day. It might be said that we're slouching towards Hades.

The author William S. Burroughs understood the city's obsession with the departed. "New Orleans," he writes in *Naked Lunch*, "is a dead museum."

But nowhere do the dead remain more present than in the city's cemeteries. "A New Orleans cemetery," the distinguished local writer Walker Percy wrote, "is a city in miniature" that can often seem "at once livelier and more exotic" than the city's other architectural achievements: its renowned sidewalk corners, verdant gardens and music clubs, which all jive and hum and bounce to their own life-affirming rhythms.

During its normal hours of operation, through frequent rainstorms and unremitting humidity, New Orleans' most notable city of the dead, St. Louis Cemetery No. 1, overflows with life. Visitors arrive by horse-drawn carriage, taxi and rockstar-sized tour bus at the cemetery's front gates, where vendors hawk bottles of water and lemonade alongside guides offering unlicensed, not to mention dubious, historical expertise. Zombie-like clusters of thirsty tourists lurch along the cemeteries' main avenues and side paths to photograph and pose alongside the aboveground vaults, most of which are tall and boxy, constructed of brick and plaster, and adorned with a simple, marble plaque.

Toward the cemetery's center, women covertly lavish lipstick kisses on the future final resting place of Nicolas Cage—yes, that Nicolas Cage—who several years ago built a nine-foot-tall, gleaming white pyramid amid a clump of crumbling, weathered crypts. In New Orleans, even the dead are not safe from gentrification.

Though New Orleanians have a deep and rich history of visiting cemeteries in order to feel more alive, the vaults at St. Louis No. 1—some of which date to the cemetery's 1789 founding—tend toward rot and decay. Families move away, die off, or, most typically, lose interest in visiting distantly related, long-dead ancestors. The local Catholic archdiocese refuses to pay for upkeep, unless a perpetual care plan has been purchased. Until recently, the cemetery operated in a sort of no man's land, sandwiched between the French Quarter's seedy backside, the long-underutilized Armstrong Park, and the now-former Iberville Housing Projects. A trip to the cemetery could quite literally result in death.

Rewatch the famous scene from *Easy Rider* when Dennis Hopper and Peter Fonda take their French Quarter escorts on a post-Mardi Gras acid trip. Between the psychedelic freak-outs and nude bodies, the camera's eye pans up, over, and around a cemetery's tombs. Some are perfectly plastered, brightly whitewashed. But most suffer from various states of disrepair: sprouting with weeds and shrubs, brittle and broken, collapsing into themselves. This is St. Louis No. 1. And it looks very much the same now as it did in the late 1960s.

It is estimated that 75 percent of the tombs in St. Louis No. 1 are orphaned. Without caretakers, the vaults are easy prey to midnight marauders, tomb raiders of marble and trinkets and bone, disturbers of the afterlife. Perhaps even more detrimental to a vault's durability is the chimerical notion, regularly perpetrated by some tour guides, that scratching a series of three *X*'s into a tomb's soft mortar exterior will result in a wish made real.

The city's most famous tomb, as well as the likely ground zero of the triple-*X* scratchiti myth, belongs to Marie Laveau. Recently, an unknown vandal painted the famous voodoo priestess's crypt a vibrant shade of pink. Whether practical joke or feminist art project, whimsy turned to angst when a local expert revealed that the latex-based paint would trap moisture inside, not allowing the vault's contents to "breathe," thus confirming that fresh air is not just for the living.

Once a month, about three dozen locals and visitors volunteer to spend their early Saturday hours tidying up the homes of the dead with Save Our Cemeteries, a nonprofit that has, since 1974, striven to preserve 13 of the city's neglected historic cemeteries through fundraising and expert-guided walking tours. The organization's home cemetery is St. Louis No. 1, where they can be most visible, do the most good, and push back against a ceaseless tide of blight.

SAD AND SHABBY, THIS TOMB WAS MUCH MORE THAN AN ORPHAN. IT WAS NAMELESS.

One breezy and blue April morning, I was tasked, together with two other volunteers, with scrubbing the exterior of a particularly ramshackle vault with a gallon-sized spray bottle of mild soapy water and a soft-bristle brush, so as not to mar the fragile plaster walls.

But the tomb needed more than a good washing. It needed a full facelift. The vault's foundation and face were cracked with scars. Plaster peeling, its bricks exposed and turning to dust, the tomb colors that of desiccated flesh. Grass grew from its top and sides. What plaster did remain was decorated with so many *XXX*'s that it resembled a cross-stitched quilt. Its marble plaque, designating who was buried within, had long been pried off and carted away—the resultant opening was crudely bricked over. Sad and shabby, this tomb was much more than an orphan. It was nameless, its anonymous owners lost to time.

I began to carefully scrub.

Though it felt entirely uplifting to volunteer a Saturday morning away, cleaning this rather unremarkable crypt selfishly clicked with the little niche I had begun to carve out for myself. In school classrooms and scholarly work, I teach and write about the chronicles of my city's past.

This volunteer opportunity was also a celebration of sorts, a chance to get outside, away from my writing desk, and just breathe. One month earlier I had successfully defended my doctoral dissertation in American history. My research focused on a now-obscure literary circle from New Orleans, a close-knit community of 19th-century poets, playwrights and pianists; novelists and journalists; historians and opera composers who promoted the idea that their city's past was exceptional, that their shared history made them different. They did not consider themselves French, though they principally spoke and wrote in that tongue. They were not impelled to call themselves Americans, yet they claimed United States citizenship and all the freedoms and failures this democracy entailed. Their tropical climate aligned more with the Caribbean than along the lines of their Confederate neighbors, while their nascent culinary and musical cultures were rooted in Africa.

They inhabited a historical and cultural middle ground, were an in-between people, exiles at home. And whether identifying as white or black or mixed-race, they often took for themselves the name "Creole," a wide-ranging word derived from the Portuguese and used to designate a New World-born descendant of Old World peoples. In their writings, these Creoles imagined themselves a united community, a Creole city, a place defined by its own uniqueness. From Twain to Faulkner, Truman to Tennessee, most every ensuing writer who would come to embrace New Orleans and its people owed a debt to these now largely untranslated, unread and forgotten authors.

Several prominent members of the literary circle were buried in this very cemetery, including its founder and spiritual godfather, Charles Gayarré. Born in 1805, the descendent of early French and Spanish settlers, Gayarré fancied himself a backwater aristocrat: an educated man, voluminous writer, and sometimes politician, born into a city where the inflated mortality rate—due to disease and violence— was inversely proportional to the population's literacy.

In a writing career that spanned eight decades, he penned novels, plays and essays for major national magazines, but it was his several volumes of history that cemented his reputation as New Orleans' first and foremost man of letters. In his bestselling chronicles, he set out to encase the city's past in what he called "a glittering frame"; to inject life into history; to compose a semi-factual narrative brimming with gilded embellishments, poetic romanticism and, at times, outright bullshit. And though he whitewashed history, fabricating names and events and dialogue, Gayarré's literary project worked. He wrote a history of this city that endures in the collective memory of its inhabitants.

Like any skillful biographer, I cultivated a knowledge of the man that could arguably rival what he knew about himself. I read his youthful writings and scoured archives for the rare unpublished jottings. I know

that at the age of 20 he fathered a son with a family slave. I possess the knowledge, loathing the fact, that he named the boy after himself, before cutting him loose and disavowing parentage for the remainder of his years. I know that he lost every penny after foolishly investing in the losing side of the Civil War. I know that he enjoyed a cup of hot chocolate in his old age. I know that it rained at his funeral.

But after spending my entire graduate student life with the man, Gayarré remained just words on a page. Alive and vivid and sharply meaningful, but still just ink. As I silently scrubbed this anonymous tomb, I imagined tracking down his mausoleum to find it in a similar state of decay. His vault would be grand, imposing, much like the life of the man whose remains it contained. But it would also be ravaged, forgotten, resembling so many other tombs scattered throughout St. Louis No. 1. By helping to restore his vault, I thought, I could get at the root of him. I could reach back into history and shake the hand of a dead man.

I scrubbed for three hours, until the *XXX*'s had faded into the faintest of scratches. I asked Save Our Cemetery's then-executive director, Angie Green, if she might know the location of the de Boré family plot—the tomb of Gayarré's mother's lineage—where I thought the man must be buried. She did not know, but told me to follow her.

We weaved through the cemetery's lanes, sidestepping tombs and tourists, searching for someone she described as St. Louis No. 1's unofficial sexton. Within minutes we ran smack into him.

He was a sturdily built man, dressed in white paint-splotched overalls and carrying a stepladder, bucket, and long-handled brush. His face was red from long hours in the sun. We had caught him hustling from one tomb to another.

"Do you maybe know where Charles Gayarré, the historian, is buried?" I asked, before even learning the stranger's name.

"Know him?" he hollered in a sharp port-of-call accent that echoes in the voices of New Orleanians. "That's my cousin!" before offering up a big, spirited hand to shake.

Still nameless, he guided me toward the back of the cemetery, near but not crossing into the "Protestant Section," where Church law once dictated that the bodies of non-Catholics be laid to rest.

"Here he is," he proudly pointed. "Charles Gayarré."

The condition of the de Boré family tomb could not have been more magnificent. I ran my fingers across the plaster's fresh coat of white paint, glittering in the sunlight. Over the carved and weather-worn letters of its marble plaques, all intact and uncracked. And along the intricate filigree of its antique wrought-iron fence and cross that guarded the vault's front, standing strong with the fine rust of age.

This was the handiwork of this same man, Ben Crowe, the Virgil to my Dante. He had only recently resealed and re-whitewashed the tomb's facade, he explained, as he had so many vaults across this cemetery. I followed him next to a nearby tomb belonging to Pierre Derbigny, a French-born patrician who became one of Louisiana's first governors, that he had also meticulously restored. A decade ago, Crowe said, his dying mother informed him of their place as a distant branch on the Derbigny family tree. He didn't believe her at first. They were a working-class family from a working-class slice of New Orleans. Nearing retirement age, he maintained bridges for the railroad and gave little thought to history. But he scoured genealogical records, tore through tattered volumes of history, and traced his family's local heritage back 11 generations, to some of the very founders of this city.

Crowe's ancestral tree flourished to include many ancient Louisiana families—Derbignys and Denises, de Borés and Lebretons—and he soon began wandering the alleys of St. Louis No. 1, searching for their final homes. Those tombs he found in disrepair, he re-plastered, repainted, rehabilitated. In his spare time and on his own dime, he soon began transferring his research, the hours spent exploring these ancient lives, onto graveside markers, hand-built but gallery quality, complete with portraits and timelines. I wanted to ask a dozen questions, but Crowe had a tough time explaining his recent obsession with the past.

I'd like to think that New Orleans is a city validated by its own clichés. The bacchanalian atmosphere, the corrupt politics and police force, the omnipresent threat of violence that runs a thin red line down every street, the beautiful rot and exquisite decay—these hackneyed tropes have existed for 300 years, because each reveals a glimmer of truth.

One last cliché might just ring true. Perhaps only in New Orleans do the dead—and undead—walk freely among the living, just as we, alive and full of spirit, move alongside the departed. For Charles Gayarré, Ben Crowe, and myself, the past tugs at every fiber of our being. Searching for life in death, we are all just chasing ghosts.

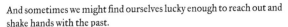

And sometimes we might find ourselves lucky enough to reach out and shake hands with the past.

I left Crowe with the promise to share my research and writing on his cousin Gayarré. He assured me that the next time he locates a relative's crypt broken and busted we will plaster and paint it together. With bucket and brush in hand, he disappeared behind a row of crypts to check on another family vault.

Before heading out of the cemetery gates, I stopped by my own adopted tomb, which now looked at least slightly cared for, and promised to visit it again.

RIEN FERTEL is a Louisiana-based writer and teacher whose work has appeared in *Garden & Gun* and *Oxford American*. He is the Lost Lit columnist for *64 Parishes* and the author of *Imagining the Creole City*, *The One True Barbecue*, and, most recently, *Southern Rock Opera*.

LABOR AND RECOVERY

Written by **KATY RECKDAHL**

I WAKE WITH the sun streaming in. My baby is nine years old, and he lies with his head on my shoulder. He crawled in with me overnight.

I watch him sleep for awhile, getting sentimental about his round face and chubby cheeks, the knees on his long legs skinned from yesterday's scooter races around the block. Once we're both up, I help him get dressed in his school uniform, dark-green pants and a white polo shirt that he tucks in, hurried and lumpy, but enough to get him past the attendance monitor.

As we drive, down North Rampart, across the Industrial Canal lift bridge, I ask him about his birthday. I ask him how he feels when Uncle Richard says to him, "Hey there, Hurricane." And when Jacques introduces him during brunch, saying "I wanted you to meet Hector. He was one of the last babies born in New Orleans before the storm."

Hector looks over at me and rolls his eyes. "Mom," he says. "This isn't an interview."

Throughout my pregnancy, I rode my bicycle around town. It didn't take much effort to pedal my big purple cruiser, since New Orleans is a flat city, except for the levees that rise up on its edges. But at a certain point, other people got nervous seeing me on that bicycle.

I understand now. I saw a pregnant woman riding her bicycle recently and she looked precarious, maybe even idiotic. But, thinking back, nearly ten years now, I remember how comfortable it was. When I walked in the thick humidity, my big baby bulge weighed on my legs and sent rivulets of sweat tumbling to my skirt's thick elastic waistband. Not so on my bicycle, which gave me a breeze even on the most humid of summer days.

My friend Tammi Fleming, a public-health whiz, instructed me to never tell anyone that I was having a boy. "Make them guess," she said. The idea was that I would keep track of guesses. The first

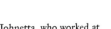

participant in Tammi's science project was Johnetta, who worked at the tiny pink launderette on Orleans Avenue and always stepped out the door to greet me as I biked home.

One day, soon after I started to show, Johnetta stuck her right hand out the door to wave, as she handed quarters to a customer with her left hand. "You're having a boy?" she yelled.

Lucky guess, I thought. But then no one was wrong. Not the clerk at the corner store, not the old Italian couple who ran the dry cleaners, not the men on the stoop in their electrician uniforms. From the way

> **"LOOK AT HOW HIGH YOU'RE CARRYING," SHE'D SAY. "DEFINITELY A BOY."**

I was carrying, all round like a basketball, people said that they knew it was a boy. [The entire time, there was only one wrong guess, from a stone-drunk neighbor who stumbled up to me, felt my stomach and slurred, "Grrrl?" Every single time I passed her, for the rest of my pregnancy, she was sure to correct herself. "Look at how high you're carrying," she'd say. "Definitely a boy."]

That's how it was, being pregnant in downtown New Orleans and riding your bicycle by the same people everyday, people who have known the baby's father all their lives. Here, what's personal can also be public.

Other musicians would warn Merv, my trumpeter boyfriend, that I could fall and hurt the baby. He wasn't really that worried about it. Sometimes, he'd laugh and roll his eyes and say, "You tell her." And they did. Constantly.

Word got to Mama Rose Glasper, the widow of Papa Joe, who operated Joe's Cozy Corner. Joe's was the bar where I showed the bartender my ultrasound to explain why I'd refused the Friday-evening Crown Royal and 7-Up that he'd poured for me when he saw me roll up on my bicycle.

One morning, Mama Rose called me and asked me to stop by and get a container of her red beans, for the baby. Her red beans are always perfect: a nice tang of green pepper with a perfect amount of hot sausage. So I arrived that night on the bicycle. She told me it was my decision. But she'd feel better if I would please ride on the *banquette*, using the French word for sidewalk. "I would never forgive myself if that baby got hurt," she said.

A few days after that, I was carrying a round watermelon home in my front bike basket when the melon rolled to the side, tipping my bike tires into the air. I jumped down and caught myself, but the bike turned sideways and clattered to the ground at my feet. Rattled, I looked around to see if any of my lecturers were watching. After that, I started taking the bus to work.

In 2005, I worked as a reporter at an alt-weekly newspaper called *Gambit*, where the small edit staff was like a big family. That spring, I had covered a lot of issues about race and culture clashing. In neighboring Jefferson Parish, I followed a tip and walked to the back of the jail complex, where sheriff's deputies were practicing their aim at handmade wooden targets painted with brown faces with big white eyes and large red lips.

New Orleans police officers had angered the city's Mardi Gras Indians by turning their St. Joseph's Night holiday into almost a raid, where officers spun their cars through the park and ordered big chiefs to remove their "fucking feathers."

When the City Council had a hearing on the matter in July, a venerated big chief, Allison "Tootie" Montana, rose to speak and began recounting the police antagonism of the Indians. Then he said, "I want this to stop," and he collapsed from a heart attack. I bicycled around the chief's neighborhood and talked to his family and people who knew him best for my *Gambit* story. I also had been doing a bunch of freelance stories, to build up money for after the baby was born. So at eight months pregnant, I covered Big Chief Tootie's funeral for *The New York Times*, which meant walking along with the two-hour funeral procession, as brass bands and Indians with drums and tambourines played and sang in their chief's honor.

The baby moved around inside me that day whenever I got close to the tuba. That happened too, on Fridays. I usually would work through the first set of Merv's gig with the Treme Brass Band. But by around 9 p.m., I would walk into Donna's Bar & Grill on North Rampart Street. As soon as he saw me, Merv would call my favorite song, "Don't forget our Monday date / That you promised me last Tuesday." Merv would be crooning and quipping and playing his horn with his bandmates and his son would be moving along, in his own way.

Merv's stagename is Kid Merv because of his great-uncle, the great trumpeter Kid Rena, who began alongside Louis Armstrong in the Colored Waifs Home for Boys. Five years before, when I had met Kid Merv, he was in his brass-band uniform: white dress shirt, black tie, black pants, white brass-band hat. It was his birthday, so people had pinned money on his chest, as is the New Orleans tradition. I pinned a five on him, told him, "Happy birthday," and kissed him on the jaw.

A few weeks later, I saw Merv in Joe's Cozy Corner and he gave me his phone number. We dated, but inconsistently, because he struggled with drinking and with cocaine and went in and out of drug rehab. Finally a musicians' program in Los Angeles seemed to work. I was turning 40 that year and we decided it was time to have a baby.

Merv always wanted a boy and he always wanted to name the boy Mervin Junior. I was less enthusiastic about yelling Merv and having two people ignore me. We finally settled on the name Hector, for Merv's father, who had died when Merv was 12.

His full name would be Mervin Hector Campbell but we would call him Hector. Though to his uncle Richard, he would be known only as "Hurricane."

About two weeks before my due date, during the last week of August 2005, I went to my weekly appointment. I was dilated a centimeter, which meant I could be moving toward labor. On the streetcar ride home, people told me that Hurricane Katrina, which had already hit Florida, was back over warm water in the Gulf of Mexico, building up for another landfall.

Soon, everyone I knew was preparing to leave town.

I'd evacuated the summer before, ahead of big Hurricane Ivan, which had turned at the last minute—as hurricanes so often do—leaving New Orleans with not even a raindrop. Like most everyone who fled Ivan, we experienced traffic so bad that a three-hour drive turned into a 12-hour nightmare. We drove with heavy eyelids, skipped meals rather than wait an hour in a fast-food drive-through, and stood in long lines for filthy filling-station restrooms with no toilet paper.

I couldn't bear the thought of going into labor in the backseat of a car stuck in evacuation gridlock. Merv agreed, saying delivering Hector himself was a no-go.

Besides, he said, we lived on Rampart Street in the French Quarter—high ground—and, if I went into labor, the city's hospitals, solid brick buildings, were some of the safest places to be during a hurricane. We decided to stay in New Orleans and take our chances.

I remember the next day like a home movie. I took a long bath, watched a doomsday news report about Katrina, and then plodded to Matassa's Market to get popsicles.

On some blocks, I had to walk in the street because so many French Quarter residents had pulled their cars onto sidewalks in front of their apartments to pack for evacuation. That was unusual. Many Quarterites took pride in not evacuating: the Quarter didn't flood and it rarely lost power for long because its below-ground electric lines, unique in New Orleans, were protected from hurricane-force winds.

New Orleans isn't known as a town run with military precision. But when a hurricane is approaching, people spring into action. I grew up in Minnesota, where you might have to grocery shop before a snowstorm and then huddle up inside with your gas-powered furnace until the storm was over and you were needed to shovel paths and dig out your car. But hurricanes require layers of preparation, far beyond wiring shutters closed or boarding up your windows.

To stay in town and do it right, you need candles, flashlights, radios, lots of batteries, charcoal for the grill, and drinking water. Sandbags, to keep water from flooding in the crack under first-floor doors. And gasoline, in case you need to evacuate. The night before, I'd been riding with a friend whose tank was three-quarters full, but he'd veered across three lanes of traffic to fill up when he saw a gas station that had gas in stock but no lines.

I'd gotten some D batteries and a jug of water. But I really wasn't in the mood to do all this preparation. I patted my stomach and told Hector we'd figure this out. Then I stopped to talk to my neighbors, old hands who were preparing for a payday. One had packed his ramshackle truck full of window-sized pieces of plywood and would work late into the night, hammering up all his boards. Another neighbor was doing a boom business, installing cable TV before the rain began. "Fill up the tub," he advised, so that I'd have water to flush the toilet if the water stopping running. I made a mental note about it. But honestly, I was still hoping that Katrina would turn away from the city.

When I got to Matassa's, I found them doing a brisk business: batteries, candles and lots of booze. "If you go into labor soon, you might be able to get to med students down the street before they tap into the whiskey they just bought," the clerk quipped.

As I walked down the pasta aisle, I felt the first pain. Like the books said, it felt distinctly different, like a band tightening around me. I walked to the register where I ran into my friend, lifelong New Orleanian L.J. Gonzales, who was there buying cigarettes. "I am not leaving town, baby," he said with disdain.

L.J. is a free spirit with a high honking laugh but regal manners, like he was teleported in from another century. So when I told him that I'd just had my first labor pain, he insisted on walking me home. I called the hospital, then Merv, who was at a gig. I called our friend Jeffrey, a tuba player, who promised he would track him down.

But Merv didn't arrive for a few hours. L.J. insisted on staying until someone could relieve him and he gamely followed instructions, pressing on the small of my back during contractions. But I could tell that he was getting increasingly nervous, as he sat in my living room, carefully leaning out an open window to light up cigarette after cigarette.

Finally, my doula arrived and L.J. gave me a kiss on each cheek and nearly sprinted out the door. We were already in the car when Merv appeared, got in the driver's seat and drove like a bat out of hell, while I perched on all fours in the back, since sitting was no longer possible.

By midnight, I was fully dilated. I started pushing, but Hector wouldn't come out. Everyone kept saying "push," but it wasn't working.

Turns out Hector's head was turned sidewise. All I could think was thank God we were not in a car somewhere. My OB reached inside me to turn him into position, which caused screeching pain. I begged for an epidural. Finally, in the wee hours of the morning, he came out, with a long skinny "banana head" from all the pushing. They rushed him to the recovery table, and I asked if I could hold him. "Let's make sure he's breathing first," said a nurse. My heart raced. Then I saw Merv, tears of joy cascading down his cheeks, as he stood over the table watching Hector's chest rise and fall with his first breaths. He looked at me and gave me a thumbs-up.

My work done, I slept most of the day. That evening, Merv weaseled in the hospital doors a few minutes after the hurricane curfew and confessed that he'd been all around town that day, bragging about our baby son.

The next morning, before dawn, the nurses woke us early. We were just getting the front edges of Katrina, but a hurricane-proof window had already broken upstairs. So they pushed all of our beds into the hallway. A new mother across the hall started screaming, a spine-tingling scream, because she'd been on the phone with her mom in the Lower Ninth Ward, who said it was already flooding badly and that she was in her attic. Then the phone had died.

Everyone looked nervous. I went to get Hector from the nursery and held him all through the storm, which sounded like an endless freight train. The power was out, but a battery-operated AM radio played at the nurses' station. Its air was filled with reports that made the city seem like the apocalypse. But we didn't see that. And whenever Merv went to the smoking area on a nearby roof, he got fairly accurate reports from staff about what was happening on the outside. We heard about the flooding. We heard there were fires and looting around town. We heard about the shelters crowded full of people in the Superdome and the convention center.

Despite that, we were happy with our beautiful boy, who was healthy, though hot to the touch, since there was no A/C and no windows that could open. We stripped him down to a diaper but he was still panting from heat. I also couldn't get him to nurse: Hector was not a natural, and I was not either. Once it was pitch black after 8 p.m., Merv would light up my nipple with his cell phone so that I could try to connect it with Hector's mouth.

Late Tuesday, Giuliana, a nurse from the hospital nursery, convinced us that Hector would sleep better in the air-conditioned room they'd set up in a far corner of the hospital, one of the last sections with a working generator.

All that night, Giuliana was helping with airlifts, as a series of helicopters rescued the sickest people and babies. Early Wednesday morning, just after the city's water faucets went dry, one mother heard that all of the babies had been airlifted. We ran down empty hallways and up stairways in a crowd to the nursery, our hearts pounding. It wasn't true. But the line between truth and rumor was so thin in those

days. I still can't explain most of that morning.

Merv came in from smoking and gathered all our things together. He told me to grab Hector. Everyone had to leave now. There was a mob of thieves headed there to get the medicine in the on-site pharmacy, a nurse said. Doctors and nurses were going from room to room, telling patients to head to the parking ramp, now. It was scary. I remember running in my slippers down the hallways, pushing Hector ahead of us in a clear plastic nursery bed.

Giuliana offered to give us a ride to Baton Rouge. There in the parking ramp, the nurses held an impromptu meeting, led by a head nurse who made sure that all other patients without cars had rides. She told us which route out of town had been cleared of storm debris, then warned that carjacking was rife. "Take off any visible jewelry and put it in your glove compartment," she said. "And, no matter what, do not stop for anyone."

As Giuliana put her car in drive, we were tense. But outside, it was quiet. Water lapped at the wheel wells, but the flooding was passable in Uptown New Orleans. The few people we saw were sitting on curbs at the edge of the street, their heads down.

It was the same way on the river bridge as we crossed it in the searing noon heat. No mobs. No one waving guns. Instead it was waves of trudging people, families with children and grandmas, in ragtag clothes, some still wet from wading through water. Those who couldn't walk were pushed in wheelchairs or even on rolling beds. Others pulled wagons or wheeled coolers with small children riding in them, followed by dirty dogs connected to owners by sagging leashes.

We searched the crowd to see if we could find our friend Jeffrey, the tuba player, and his family. I couldn't stop crying. As we drove out of the city toward Baton Rouge, we looked for the caravan of buses that was slated to take this same road into town by the end of that day. We didn't see a single bus.

On the way, we got our first cell-phone signal. I had barely any juice in my phone, so I called my sister Beth in Phoenix. She's a clutch in chaotic situations. "I'll call a travel agent and get you here to Phoenix," Beth said firmly. "Then I'll call Mom."

Beth said that Mom and Dad had been worried sick, glued to the TV, looking for us in every New Orleans report. That morning, they had been debating driving their minivan from Minnesota to New Orleans, to pick us up at the hospital. Beth laughed. "But don't call now. She won't hear the phone, because she's drying her hair, getting ready for all the news reporters that are headed to the house to talk about you."

Soon Beth called back, breathlessly. "You're booked for a flight from Baton Rouge to Phoenix on Friday—it's the best we could do," she said. "Can you wait at the airport until then?"

It was Wednesday. I felt smelly and ratty as we stood in the airport reservations line with Hector and our "luggage," a light-blue hospital trash bag. The man in front of us paid for his flight from a wad of bills. At the next counter, a woman tried to pay with a series of credit cards, none of them working. But Beth had come through. We checked in two days early. The reservations clerk advised us to head to the gate.

When we got to security, a woman looked down at the baby seat and frowned, then walked from the scanner to me. "How old is that baby?" she asked. I panicked, remembering something about infants not being able to fly until a certain age.

"He's three days old," I said. "We just came from the hospital in New Orleans."

She nodded, then motioned to everyone ahead of us in line. "Everyone—please move out of the way," she said. "There's an infant here." I told her thank you and she touched my arm. "When you get to the gate, sit down," she said. "Your color looks awful."

The gate crew saw Hector and got us on the next plane to Atlanta. On the connecting flight to Phoenix, the pilot announced that there was a new Katrina baby from New Orleans on board that night's flight and everyone applauded.

None of us remembers rain while we were in Phoenix. It seemed like outer space there, with the soaring red cliffs and the canyons, the air that left your nose feeling like it had dried glue inside. We spent nearly a year out west. A lot of that time is blurry to me now. Hector's erratic feeding and sleeping schedules. Negotiating with FEMA and Red Cross and finding loved ones. Our phones were nearly worthless. The building that controlled the 504 area code for cell phones had been submerged. Sometimes you could get a daytime call, but usually it was too jammed. Often we'd get late-night calls, relaying word that someone else was out of New Orleans and safe. Or not.

My sister Beth shuttled us around and fed us at first. Within the first few weeks, Valley Presbyterian Church in Scottsdale called to sponsor us, setting up an apartment furnished with everything from pots and pans to a handmade baby quilt to a pair of slippers for me next to the bed. Merv's bandmates from the Treme Brass Band also ended up in Phoenix, thanks to the same church and a jazz group. Fred Sheppard, a gangly older saxophonist who had played with Otis Redding, Ray Charles and Fats Domino, spent hours holding Hector, who was always content with Shep. Turns out Shep would scat in his ear to calm him.

The tuba player, Jeffrey, and his wife Ann ended up living by us in Scottsdale. As we crossed the river bridge on that Wednesday, they had been walking through floodwaters to the convention center; they had left on foot two days later when the children became so dehydrated that they were shaking. A renegade city bus driver stopped on the bridge, opened her doors, and drove them and a busload of other evacuees to safety a few hours away.

Jeffrey's Scottsdale house had a pool, but the closest his son would go was a lawnchair at its edge, where he'd sit with his little Spiderman towel.

Merv also seemed shaken by the storm in a way that I couldn't understand. It was as though he felt invincible, beyond sobriety. People bought him drinks as a way of welcoming the new trumpeter from New Orleans, and he eagerly gulped them down.

I no longer saw his gigs. Hector was going through a colicky time, and I often spent hours walking the neighborhood like a zombie, lulling him to sleep. A few hours later, Merv would undo my work, as he stumbled in, loaded and loud.

Merv still had penitent moments, but I was done. On Mother's Day, I had the locks changed. I applied for a year-long, post-Katrina journalism fellowship and I got it. A month later, my friend Munce flew into town to help me pack up a car and a U-Haul trailer on my own. We rode back toward New Orleans in a caravan with Jeffrey and Ann and their family. Merv stayed behind.

We drove for 12 hours at a time, up and down mountains in Arizona and then across the width of Texas. Hector hated his carseat then and screamed whenever he wasn't sleeping, unless someone sat next to him. So Munce drove almost nonstop.

Early in the drive, as we climbed up a steep Arizona incline, a car sidled up next to us and pointed to the U-Haul trailer hitch, which had come loose and was hanging by one wire. Jeffrey bought wire and a chain from a nearby gas station and fixed it by the side of the road.

The next day, Jeffrey's big rental truck stalled in the middle of the mountains. U-Haul brought us a new one hours later, but we had to unload and reload the whole thing in the middle of an asphalt parking lot.

Finally, 11 months after we'd left, we drove back into New Orleans. My friend Carol had been staying at my place on Rampart while her roof was repaired, so our apartment was clean and felt like a time capsule, ready for the infant who no longer fit the clothes laid out for him.

Munce took a cab to the airport, back to Minneapolis. I put Hector in the stroller and took a walk through the French Quarter, back to Matassa's, where owners Louie and John Matassa greeted him like their own child.

At that point, nearly a year after the storm, Hector was one of the few babies in town, a novelty of sorts. I'm not a punctual person, but during that time, I had to leave the house about 20 minutes early so that I could give people time to grab Hector's chubby leg in the stroller or—if I knew them—to hold him and kiss him on his cheek.

My neighbors concluded that Hector had basically planned the whole thing. "Have you met Hector?" they'd ask someone new. "He was born up at Touro just before the storm. He was determined to be a New Orleans baby."

Jeffrey's family had settled for the time being in Houston, near some of Ann's family. He would commute to New Orleans to play gigs on weekends and would sleep on my couch. But it was several months until I saw the rest of the Phoenix crew again.

It was a somber meeting, a funeral for Shep, who hadn't told anyone he was sick and was found dead in his Phoenix apartment. I wrote the paper's obituary for him, my vision blurry with tears. His ashes were flown to New Orleans for the funeral service, which ended —as is the custom for musicians—with a large traditional second-line procession. His niece walked out front holding a framed photo of him with his saxophone, his gray hair puffing out from under his trademark leather baseball cap.

I carried Hector through the procession. It was raining lightly, and New Orleans evacuees who had driven to the funeral from all parts of the South were following the band, dancing and monkeyshining for Shep. He may have died alone, they said, but he wasn't going to be put down alone.

Hector couldn't stop watching the drummers. He'd fuss whenever I turned away from the drumline, often to hug someone whom I hadn't seen since before the storm. When we got back to the church, Fatman, a snare drummer, handed Hector his drumsticks as a gift. As rain dripped onto us, Hector stood on the ground and reached toward Fatman's snare. Tap tap tap.

Fatman was overjoyed: I remember his big grin as he walked us to the car, with Hector still drumming even as I strapped him into his car seat. Then Hector tapped the sticks on the back of my headrest, all the way home to Rampart Street.

KATY RECKDAHL is a New Orleans-based journalist and frequent contributor to *The Times-Picayune* | *New Orleans Advocate*, WDSU television and *The New York Times*.

BARBARIN BOYS AND WALTER BLUE'S DEATH

Written by **DANNY BARKER**

ALL [MY GRANDFATHER] ISIDORE BARBARIN'S FOUR SONS, Paul, Louis, Lucien and William, were playing and starting to get on the jazz whirl. So naturally I was entangled in this scene. I couldn't escape: all they did was talk, play, dream, eat, sleep, argue, follow music—jazz that is. They knew and discussed everything that was happening about jazz. During the period 1916 to 1920 there was a big demand for jazz musicians. If there was to be a jazz affair in the immediate neighborhood I followed my younger uncles Willie and Lucien to the scene, and watched and listened as they commented on who was playing [good, great, bad or lousy]. And they knew jazz. Then I began to hear of the great musicians. They talked of who was away, up North or East, doing great. Who was going away. Who came back.

Sidney Bechet was the topic of much discussion. He would write his family who lived near, a couple of blocks away. They knew when he was in New York City, Chicago, Paris, London, Russia, Germany. I heard tales of how he created so much excitement, admiration and fame for his playing. Nobody at that time was spoken of with the same level of sensation as Sidney Bechet. Listening of Bechet's travels and the great demand for New Orleans musicians who could play well caused me to decide to become a musician.

With Willie and Lucien I began to follow around the neighborhood. I began to absorb what was happening. They were nice to me, their little nephew, who was so naive and curious. I asked question on top of question and got answers on top of answers: the smart and right answers. Don't do this; stay away from there; that's bad; that was good; watch and keep your guard and defense up; that's our friend; they are no good; they look for trouble; if they hit you, tell us, we'll get 'em later.

The first day I went to public school, which was a supposedly rough school in the eighth ward [I lived in the seventh ward], my two uncles played hookey from their school, came by and got in a friendly huddle with the tough bunch at my school. I was introduced to the leaders, who said they would look out for me, which they did from the third grade to the eighth grade. When I graduated I was one of the boys. I was very popular in school, particularly because the larger boys and those who loved music knew that I was related to so many musicians, and they saw me at many social affairs.

When there were music arguments and discussions about who was the greatest they would call me to settle the argument. Many of the school children had relations who played music. When I came to school playing the ukulele I was instantly a celebrity. I started jazz sessions that would get out of hand: swinging, hand-clapping, happy scenes at twelve o'clock, until the stern, serious Miss Fannie Williams, the principal, called me to her office and put a stop to that. She told me not to bring the ukulele to school again.

My uncle Lucien, my mother's brother, was a smart, clever, nerveless youngster, who was active as a bumblebee. He would try anything, would get into things and talk his way out. He was the commander of us three: me and Willie. He would say, "Let's make kites!"

"Let's go to work!"

"Let's go junking!"

"Let's go look for money!"

"Let's go to the bayou!"

"Let's go to the lake!"

"Let's go in the woods!"

"Let's go get blackberries!"

"Let's go by Mrs. Barker and get some biscuits!"

"Let's go to the French Market and get some specs!"

"Let's go watch Jeff Holloway!"

"Let's go hop a freight train!"

And off we would go following Lucien.

Willie and Lucien were forever whistling, imitating the different cornet and clarinet players of that time. They both had good memories of the playing styles of many popular musicians. They would challenge each other: "Whistle like Buddy Petit."

"Whistle like Big Eye Louis."

"Whistle like Manuel Perez."

"Whistle like Walter Blue."

If Lucien said, "Let's go to work," it meant that he had passed some place and saw that some chore or light work was needed: like a pile of bricks out on the sidewalk, a load of sand, some light lumber—things that boys could move. When this happened, Lucien did the business and paid us off equally. It was not because we were hungry or poor—no. He liked to have some money, always.

My stepfather and uncles' bakers' wagon would drop off hot fresh French bread every day without fail. All branches of the family believed in eating, and eating enough. The pots on all the family stoves were full or half-full of something good to eat. No jive cooks for this family and its relatives. All the children just had to mention about being hungry and they were promptly fixed a large sandwich, and their young friend also received one. It was sacrilege to have hungry children with empty stomachs around.

Now if we went junking, we each got burlap or flour sacks which were always around, and we walked the neighborhood streets picking up bottles, rags, metals—zinc, brass, copper, lead—anything that could be used second-hand. We would see articles and things of all sorts in people's yards. We would knock on the door and ask for the objects: old beds, old chairs. We made wagons with large, heavy wheelbarrow wheels and hauled the things to a junk-shop, where Lucien bargained [generally successfully], and then there was the equal split-up of money.

If he said, "Let's go look for money!" OK. We three walked a street. Lucien walked the right side scanning the gutter, street and sidewalk; Willie walked the left side, slowly, doing likewise; and I walked the center. Our six sharp, keen eyes missed no area, and we found money almost every time.

We often went to the large French Market to get specs, as overripe fruits and vegetables were humorously called. The large French Market is about four blocks long. We went to the wholesale section, where the produce was bought, sold, sorted and delivered. There were always the tables where the overripe and spoiled stuff was put. My uncles would somehow always ask the right man for some specs and almost immediately with their pocket knives would start cutting off the bruised or spoiled part and eating the different fruits as if they were famished, and I would join them. We would eat until we got stuffed and short-winded and then slowly walk home. That was fun for me, but I wondered, sort of scared, what would happen if any of the Barkers had seen me doing this savage devouring of this supposedly rotten fruit. We would eat peaches, pears, plums, bananas, oranges, pineapples, mangoes, grapes, all varieties of summer fruits.

My grandfather Mr. Barker liked fruit, but only bought the choicest, the best, from the first-class stands in the market, and there was always a large bowl of sweet-smelling fruit near his kitchen—no specs. He bought giant ripe sweet watermelons and cantaloupes that we feasted on. He knew about melons, which ones to pick from a large pile. So while I gorged myself with specs with my young uncles I looked about at the people cautiously, so that I could duck or hide or quickly turn away my face and head in case a Barker or someone who knew them should see me eating specs like an orphan or pickaninny, as colored youngsters who did such things were called.

Lucien was a great persuader. He could talk his way out of rumbles with other youngsters. But not Willie—he had a quick, violent temper. When we met up with young roughnecks and it looked like trouble, while Lucien argued, compromised, appeased and conned the enemy, Willie and I looked about for weapons. Willie picked up anything that he could lift that would wound, maim, kill, cripple. Then he went furiously into battle. Be it a stave, brick, bottle, bucket, large plank, board, iron pipe—anything lethal he would see quickly at hand. He was accused of having a quick temper by the family and most of the youngsters in the neighborhood. He seriously believed, "Fight first, fuss after." When his anger built up inside until he started crying and the blood vessels bulged, he was almost physically uncontrollable. Grown folks—men—had to take hold of him. He was ready to die in combat if he thought that you were taking advantage of him or someone close to him.

There were few paved streets then, and on the mud streets there lay small cobblestones, oyster shells of various sizes, broken bricks of many sizes and pieces of broken bottles [the bottoms that did not crush easily]. When Willie was walking in the street looking down for money he practiced throwing these missiles at targets, and was a sharpshooter or marksman. Many times we would gather in open lots playing marbles or tops. Willie was champ at these skilled games. We would also stand up empty bottles like pins in a bowling alley and use baseball-sized stones for balls, pitching at the bottles from a distance about fifty feet away. Willie was the champ at crashing the group of bottles in all directions.

Then some days Lucien would say, "Let's go to Mrs. Barker and get some hot biscuits!" OK. We walked to 1027 Chartres Street, through the long alley into the large yard, up the long steep stairs to my grandmother's kitchen. There we were greeted like long-lost wayfaring prodigal sons. The Barkers, being from the country and not influenced by anything French, never served store-bought bread, that is French or white bread. The family ate homemade bread, biscuits, cornbread, corn muffins, which my grandmother cooked. She used Ballard flour, which was the best biscuit flour at that time. Now her cooking was different from my grandmother's cooking. Lucien and Willie's mother cooked in the French fashion, my other grandmother cooked country-style. This country cooking was new to my two uncles and they much loved it. Mrs. Barker knew what we wanted and would oblige with her food, which was always plentiful. First she would hurriedly make a large pan of wonderful fluffy biscuits. And then there was the dessert: jars of preserves like watermelon rinds, peaches, apples. Then the large jar of molasses for the biscuits: hot biscuits and butter—the best. We ate until every biscuit had disappeared. I would naturally get uneasy or restless, but Lucien the promoter used to smile and say, "Thank you ma'am, Mrs. Barker, for the nice dinner," and I would kiss everybody. We would walk lazily back to the Barbarin residence, and there my uncles would relate in details about the great feast, especially the big pan of biscuits.

At that time I was too small to hang in the company of Louis and Paul Barbarin, the two older boys, who were young men. The larger brothers by then had decided to become musicians—drummers. They were going through the frustrating musician's apprenticeship, which was especially tough in New Orleans. This strict period was trying on a young musician who was just beginning, because there were so many youngsters grabbing up musical instruments. One of the bitter experiences you had to tolerate in silence was that the old veterans saw to it that a youngster did not get a big head, or that his reputation did not exceed his ability. No matter how well you mastered your instrument in the presence of these veteran pros, the comment was always the same, "Some day that boy is going to make a good musician." This "some day" business was very unnerving, especially after you had sat in one of the many jazz bands, played well, maybe sensationally, and shook up the listening public. Then you would hear this "some day" statement, said with apparently indifferent expression. But if you looked at the older band members' faces, you could see expressions of contempt, jealousy and fear—of a potential rival.

There was one musician, Sidney Bechet, who as a youngster would come into one of the many dance halls unexpectedly, with empty hands, but with his clarinet apart and three separate bits each in a separate pocket. The usual crowd standing looking and listening at the band and its soloists would applaud, whistle and implore the young Bechet to play. He usually did. Slowly he took the parts of the clarinet and joined them together His keen musical ear gave him as close a tuning as possible. Then he waited politely until the leader ot the band signaled, "Take it!" Then Bechet proceeded to play his own great jazz improvisations to the amazement of the audiences.

On one occasion I was there, second lining, beside the Perseverance Benevolent Mutual Aid Association. It was a Sunday morning at about 11 a.m., and this well-organized society of men were having their annual street parade celebrating one of many past anniversaries. There were two brass bands, the Onward and another, I don't recall the name. My young uncles [who knew all the musicians like boys knew baseball stars and teams] mentioned that Walter Blue was in the other brass band. I planned to second line for a few blocks out of sight of my grandfather, who was in the Onward band and forbade all of his boys to second line because it was dangerous on occasions. Police on horseback would sometimes chase the large second line to keep them under control and out of the path of the parade, as their presence was annoying the society members.

I followed my uncles through the crowd of hundreds of spectators, right by the side of the other band and Walter Blue. The band struck up and the parade started. We followed, bouncing along to the great-sounding music and watching the playing and sound of Walter Blue. Then I remember two members of the band taking hold of Walter Blue and helping him to a stoop on the sidewalk. He was laid down and the crowd closed in around the stoop. I tried to get through to

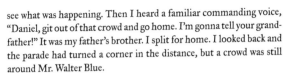

see what was happening. Then I heard a familiar commanding voice, "Daniel, git out of that crowd and go home. I'm gonna tell your grandfather!" It was my father's brother. I split for home. I looked back and the parade had turned a corner in the distance, but a crowd was still around Mr. Walter Blue.

Later that day the news spread that Walter Blue died while playing the parade. He had eaten in the corner barroom three pickled eggs and some whiskey. After starting to blow his horn, the pickled eggs and whiskey came up and choked him to death. The people who assisted him to the porch should not have laid him down on his back—they should have sat him upright. Walter Blue was a great blues player. He never was given his proper acclaim.

DANNY BARKER (1909–1994) was an elder statesman of jazz and an international representative of New Orleans and Black culture. This excerpt comes from his 1986 memoir, *A Life in Jazz*, filled with his memories of musical greats such as Jelly Roll Morton, Cab Calloway and Dizzy Gillespie, alongside his personal struggles, triumphs, escapades and musings. Reprinted with permission from The Historic New Orleans Collection.

INDEX

INDEX